Managing Cross-Cultural Transition

Steven Shepard

Managing Cross-Cultural Transition:
A Handbook for Corporations, Employees, and Their Families

Steven Shepard

ALETHEIA
Publications

Shepard, Steven
Managing cross-cultural transition: a handbook for corporations, employees, and their families

Copyright © 1998 by Steven Shepard

All rights reserved. No portion of this book may be reproduced, by any process or technique, without the express written consent of the publisher.

Library of Congress Catalog Card Number: 97-72339
ISBN: 0-9639260-5-5

Copyeditor: Leslie Bernstein
Cover design: Jackie Frant
Interior design and composition: Guy J. Smith
Photo of author by Martin LaVallee

Aletheia Publications
38-15 Corporal Kennedy St.
Bayside, NY 11361

Printed in Canada
10 9 8 7 6 5 4 3 2 1

*This book is dedicated with love
to my parents, who took me overseas,
and to Sabine, Cristina, and Steven,
who make it a joy to be home.*

Acknowledgments

A book like this relies on the contributions of many people. For professional expertise in the area of repatriation and its impact on the individual, the family, and the employer, I am indebted to the following individuals: Linda Oleson, support services officer, Family Liaison Office, U.S. Department of State; Kristine A. Stuart, manager of human resources planning and policies, Chevron Overseas Petroleum, Inc.; Douglas E. Martin, home office director, McDonald's International; Norma McCaig, founder, Global Nomads International; Douglas S. Rice, Ph.D., consultant, LSI Litigation Sciences, Inc.; my brothers, Roger and John Shepard, who shared the Spanish experience with me; Dave Train, Hill Associates; David Graves, Weyerhaeuser Corporation; Steve Pyrek, IRS Press Office; Juanita Mortimer, Bureau of Economic Analysis, U.S. Department of Commerce; Dale Pederson, Airtouch Communications, formerly with Pacific Telesis International; Richard Bahner, global human resources director, AT&T; Mona Melanson, Meredith McClanahan, and Susan Musich, United States Peace Corps Office of Returned Volunteer Services; Nedra Hardzel, career development and transition consultant; Cathleen Dargy, Bank of America; Jean Dennison, NYNEX; Dr. Frank Alagna, Consultants for International Living; Deborah Schott and John Phelps, Southwestern Bell Corporation; Doug Ripley, ADC Corporation; Walter and Millie Woolf, Air Animal®;

Jerry Hanley; Prudential Relocation Services; Windham International; SRI Selection Research International; Craighead Publications; Inlingua; William Sheridan, National Foreign Trade Council; and many current and former expatriates who chose not to be identified.

From the American School of Madrid's alumni ranks, I am indebted to Bob Cullen, Kari Kolstad-Lengierre, Debbie White, Bob Verlaque, Michael Sellmer, Joe Rue, Joe Rodriguez, Manuel Quirós, Patty Marquart-Ikenberry, Keith Lessig, Joan King, Dave Graves, Steve Dreisler, Carolyn Casey, Sissy Bikkal, and Jorge Balandrin. ¡Saludos!

For assistance with the manuscript, I relied heavily on Bill Malmi, whose editorial rapier enhanced the readability of the book immensely; Gary Kessler, director of information technology at Hill Associates and an accomplished writer in his own right; Mark Fei, a senior member of technical staff with Hill Associates and a former expatriate himself; Mike Lawler, also a member of technical staff with Hill Associates; my parents, whose many years abroad provided a sanity check; my friend and critic, Dennis McCooey; and my wife, Sabine, whose editorial insights and love kept me going.

For psychic inspiration, I relied on the timeless music of Jon Anderson, Bill Bruford, Rick Wakeman, Steve Howe, and Chris Squire, known to the world as Yes. May you play forever.

Finally, I am, as always, forever indebted to my wonderful kids, Cristina and Steven, who continue to put up with my wild ramblings and provide me with a loving home to return to and a reason to keep doing what I do.

CONTENTS

Introduction	1
Part 1: The Multinational Corporation	15
Outbound	20
Inbound	22
Statistics of Success—or Failure	25
Part 2: Employee Assessment and Selection	34
Employee Selection	38
Line Management versus HR	38
Employee Factors	40
Spouse Concerns	41
Health	44
Age and Maturity	46
Other Pitfalls	47
Part 3: Preparation and Expatriation	64
Predeparture Orientation	65
Preparation and Counseling	69
The Mentor	70
The Mentor's Responsibilities	71
Most Important: Communication	72
Formal Mentor Programs	74
Letters of Understanding	78
Domestic Housing	80
Employees: Remember the Family	85
Part 4: In-Country Transition	94
Arrival	95
Settling In	96
Acceptance	98
First Home Leave: Satisfaction and Conflict	99

Two-Career Families	101
Part 5: Reentry	105
Preparation for Reentry	108
The Repatriation Process	110
Breaking Ground: The Domestic Workplace	119
Professional Transition	122
Part 6: The Special Case of Expatriate Children	132
Five Phases of the Global Nomad	139
Preparing Children for Reentry	141
The Five Cs	149
Part 7: Creating a Multinational Employee Management Strategy	157
Issues, Concerns, and Special Cases	164
Interorganizational Transfers	164
Turnabout: Educating the Home Office	165
Putting the Skills to Work	168
Operational Skills	168
Tactical Skills	170
Strategic Skills	172
Peer Counseling and Family Support	175
Compensation Issues	176
Intangible Components of Compensation	180
Foreign Business Practices	182
Fiscal Responsibilities of the Expatriate Employee	186
Feedback	193
Keys to Managing the Expatriate Employee	199
Conclusion	214
Bibliography	217

Glossary	220
Appendix	225
Organization List	225
Useful Contacts	229
Online Resources	230
Permissions	232
Index	235
About the Author	240

Expatriate: **ex•pa•tri•ate** *n.* One who has taken up residence in a foreign country. *–v.* To remove (oneself) from residence in one's native land.

Repatriate: **re•pa•tri•ate** *tr.v.* To restore or return to the country of birth, citizenship, or origin.

American Heritage Dictionary, Third Edition

Introduction

When I began this project, I didn't realize that I was writing a book. I was, in fact, searching for an explanation for certain long-standing feelings and behaviors that were a part of my behavioral makeup and that I didn't understand. The more I learned, though, the more compelled I felt to continue. Before I knew it, I had the beginnings of a healthy manuscript. I also realized that I was not the only person attempting to deal with the feelings that were driving me.

Late in 1968 my father, a petroleum geologist, was transferred to Spain. With great trepidation and excitement my mom, brothers, and I packed up our west Texas household, boarded a 707 in New York City, and followed my father to Madrid to begin what were to be the most memorable five years of my life.

We were reasonably well prepared for the experience. Prior to the move we collected dozens of books on Spain and western Europe and devoured them. We learned everything there was to know about the country's culture, language, food, and people. We sought out people who had vacationed there and introduced ourselves to Spanish students who were living in our town for the equivalent of a "junior year abroad" program. By the time we left we knew what to expect in the way of housing, schooling, and health care. As a result, we were not overly shocked by what we found in our new country, and before we knew it we had "gone native," to use a term of the time. We fit in, we had Spanish friends, we spoke the language. We were *comfortable* there. We liked it. We were home.

In 1972 I graduated from the American School of Madrid and left Spain to return to college in the States. Once the initial euphoria of having root beer, Mexican food, and more than two TV channels available to me faded away, I began to realize that I was something of a social misfit. I didn't understand the members of my stateside peer group, and they didn't understand me. When asked about my experiences, I told them about the only things I could—bullfights, soccer games, Sunday flea markets.

I was branded a braggart and show-off, titles I didn't deserve. Understand: I wasn't any better than my stateside peers; I was just different. *Very* different. My experiences weren't the same as theirs, and vice versa. In the end I retreated and stopped talking about my childhood experiences in Spain. I withdrew to the sidelines and soon found that in some ways I had become an observer of life rather than an active participant in it.

This phenomenon, I discovered, isn't limited to expatriate *children*. When the rest of my family returned from Spain my father found it difficult to fit in at the office. He was fine when in a group of other "ex-expatriates," but when forced to interact with domestic peers he was the proverbial fish out of water. My mom, uprooted from the chaotic, exciting life of an expatriate, found it almost impossible to join the local social scene. Both she and my father had difficulty forming friendships, as did most of their friends who had returned from overseas assignments.

In fact, the tight-knit expatriate community *remained* an expatriate community, even in California. Years later my parents were offered the opportunity to return to an overseas post, and they jumped at it. Yes, there were financial incentives; they were going to Yugoslavia, after all, an Eastern Bloc hardship post that was financially very rewarding. But they later confirmed that they left eagerly because it was an opportunity to get back to the world in which they felt most comfortable.

Years later, in the summer of 1992, I attended my twentieth high school reunion. It was held in White Plains, New York, because the New York City area was roughly equidistant between the American School of Madrid and the thirty-some-odd graduates who had scattered to all the corners of the earth following graduation.

The reunion was a resounding success. It went on for three days and only ended because people had to catch flights back to their far-flung homes. Strange: at no time did that typical moment arrive when, after all the stories had been told, the catching up done, and the nostalgic memories reviewed, everyone lapsed into awkward silence. Not even twenty years of separation could calm this group, a fact that at the time I found somewhat odd.

During the second evening's festivities, the group gathered at the home of one of the graduates, where we retreated into the study to continue a conversation that had begun over dessert. I had asked the group what kinds of things they had done and what had happened to them when they left Spain following graduation. The questions were asked innocently enough, but the responses (including my own) were electrifying. Virtually without exception, they were identical.

We all wandered a lot, both emotionally and physically. We had trouble "becoming somebody." We didn't fit in when we came back, and spent a lot of time trying to recapture the kinship, the closeness, the culture that we left behind. Many of us became superachievers in an attempt to overcome our feelings of aimlessness and "disconnectedness." Our class yielded an inordinately high percentage of doctors, lawyers, high-tech entrepreneurs, even a few successful politicians.

Many of us returned to Spain, some repeatedly. Some waited until after college; others took time off between semesters to make the pilgrimage. We were looking for something, but most of us didn't really know what it was at the time. It was an intangible, ephemeral thing, yet deep inside us it was as real as a hammer blow.

During the conversation I began to realize that we were unusual people. We knew the Prado Museum and could speak intelligently about Velasquez and his contemporaries and compare notes on painting techniques. We spoke at least two languages fluently and were vastly tolerant of different races, cultures, societies. We ate squid and octopus and blood sausage without a second thought, and were comfortable when placed in virtually any social situation.

I have to admit that I took solace in the discovery that I was not alone, that others experienced the same feelings of "not belonging" when they repatriated. I found, almost without exception, that they all suffered from the same symptoms when they returned to their home country: They didn't fit in; they didn't get along with others; they felt underutilized, minimally challenged at work or school, and bored.

I came away from the reunion energized and refreshed, content in the realization that I wasn't "broken"—or at least if I was, I was one of many. The desire to write this book welled up from somewhere deep inside after that, driven by a need to discover more about this phenomenon that I dubbed *expatriosis*—also called *reverse culture shock.*

I read everything I could find on the subject, but that wasn't enough. To expand my comprehension of the impact of cross-cultural transition, I interviewed corporate global human resources managers;

expatriates; former expatriates; children of current and former expatriates; and directors of professional support organizations. Somewhere along the line I turned introspective and began to realize that many of my own behavioral characteristics undoubtedly stem from my years in Spain.

From that moment on, the writing became painful and revealing. On the one hand, I learned things about myself that were humorous, enlightening, sometimes embarrassing, but always valuable. I found, for example, that I match the global nomad profile, discussed in Part 6, in uncanny ways. It does indeed take me five minutes to answer the simple question, "Where are you from?"

Following expatriation, the stages I went through were typical. When I first arrived in Madrid I longed for home (Texas), for my friends, for all things both familiar and comfortable. That sense of isolation and "disconnectedness" lasted many months, but at some point along the way something fundamental shifted. Texas was no longer home; Aravaca was. I began to speak Spanish, made Spanish friends, and learned to play soccer and *futbolín* and dance to Spanish music. The boxy Spanish shoes and ill-fitting clothes that I had once gawked at no longer looked odd; I even began to wear them myself. And every once in a while, wandering through the flea market or clicking across the cold cobbles of the Plaza Mayor or preparing to watch a bullfight, I would hear the loud, abusive-sounding tones of an American tourist and I would feel...ashamed. It was a strange but somehow satisfying feeling. I didn't want to be associated with tourists because they were embarrassing. I didn't want to have to explain their behavior.

I was becoming multicultural. A global nomad.* A third culture kid. I didn't know it, and I wouldn't know it until several years later, when I went to college.

Because we had moved to Spain from west Texas, I enrolled in a Texas university following graduation so that I would be able to visit relatives on holidays (I couldn't fly off to Spain every time a long weekend came along). So in June 1972 I graduated from the American School of Madrid, hopped on a plane, flew to Texas, and enrolled at Texas Tech University. My first inkling that I was "different" came when a student in a chemistry class asked me if Madrid was near Dallas. Farther east, I replied.

A year and a half later I transferred to the University of California at Berkeley. My family had moved to the San Francisco Bay area from Spain shortly after I left for college, and since they were now residents, I qualified for in-state tuition at Berkeley.

One realization that I had while writing this book was that, with the exception of people I knew in Texas before we moved to Spain and who also enrolled at Texas Tech, I am not in contact with a single person from either of the two undergraduate universities I attended. *Not one.* I am, however, in

---

* From Global Nomads International, Inc. Global nomads are defined as children who grow up outside their passport country as a result of their parents' occupation. They are neither members of their passport country's culture nor members of the host country. They are somewhere in between. An alternative term often used for these children is *third culture kid*.

close contact with many people from the American School of Madrid. Why?

That's a question I pondered for a long time. Now, of course, the answer is obvious. I didn't have anything in common with my stateside peers; we had nothing to talk about. We couldn't share high school memories, weekend activities, or hobbies. While they talked football, I talked soccer. While they rallied around rock, I listened to flamenco. When they craved burgers, I craved chorizo, and on and on. The more we got to know each other, the further apart we drifted. I learned to distance myself, to keep quiet, to play a passive, onlooker-only role. I watched, and I learned.

I graduated from Berkeley with a degree in...Spanish, of course. I wasn't sure what I wanted to do with my life, but I knew that I wanted to do something that involved travel, especially if the travel included Spain. In fact, I made two pilgrimages to Spain after graduation, each for several months. At the time I told friends and family, and even convinced myself, that I was making these trips to investigate graduate school at the University of Madrid; now I realize that they were actually attempts to get back to the world in which I was most comfortable. Each time, I returned to California energized.

I finally settled down and entered the job market. I certified as a SCUBA instructor, opened a dive shop with a friend, and immediately had business cards printed that advertised bilingual instruction. I wrote a book on SCUBA diving, translated it into Spanish, and even taught a few Spanish-speaking students. Several years later I married my wife, Sabine, who is German.

Eventually I went to work for Pacific Bell, spending ten years with them. At one point I was transferred to Pacific Telesis International, where I worked on a project in Venezuela, translating documents between English and Spanish and serving as an interpreter. That was a career high point. Another came years later when I was assigned to telephone company strike duty in Los Angeles, translating requests for assistance from Spanish to English for operators.

In 1991 I left Pacific Bell, moved to Vermont, and went to work for Hill Associates as a writer and teacher of telecommunications courses. In many ways it is the ideal job for me. I travel a great deal and teach in cities all over the United States. I have taught in Spanish in Mexico City, and have traveled to Europe and Asia on business. Everywhere I go I meet interesting people. The job assuages my wanderlust and slakes my ongoing hunger to meet new people from exotic places—even if those exotic places are Omaha, Phoenix, Los Angeles, and New Haven.

It's a well-known fact that almost all medical students go through a period during which they imagine themselves to be suffering from the symptoms of the very diseases they study. As I make observations about myself, I have to be careful that I am not falling into the trap of seeing so much of the expatriate model in myself because I know so much about it. After interviewing many people, however, I have found that this is not the case. My perceived behaviors are real, not imagined, and are widespread throughout the community of people who have lived overseas.

Some of them are humorous; all are interesting. For example, I am a self-contained traveler. I carry a bag that contains everything I could ever need should I suddenly have to drop everything and go. The things in that bag also define who I am: a passport; a tape recorder for interviews; a laptop computer; an Audubon nature calendar; a compass; a short-wave radio; a flashlight. Research materials for whatever articles, courses, or books I happen to be working on at the time. Be prepared: the Boy Scout from Hell!

What else? I hate good-byes. I cry when I have to say good-bye. When we have company, I will do anything I can to avoid having to face a person as they leave. I'd much prefer to have an unavoidable reason to call and say good-bye from the office, or better yet, from another city. And when I'm the one who travels, my mind leaves hours before my body gets on the airplane. Just ask my wife. How many times have I heard her say, "You're gone already, aren't you?" What can I say? It's a defense mechanism. I've had to do it too many times.

But what of the good things that have come from my childhood in Spain? There are so many. I am immensely tolerant and forgiving. In crowds I seek out foreigners and gravitate to the sounds of exotic languages that I don't understand. I love the music of language, any language. I am fascinated by diverse religious teachings and am equally comfortable in a

Zen retreat, a Southern Methodist fried chicken dinner prayer service, a Jewish Seder, or the chanting liturgy of Catholicism rumbling through a massive cathedral. I love to read, especially travel essays like those of William Least Heat-Moon, Bill Bryson, Pico Iyer, and Paul Theroux.

Again, I'm not alone. I have talked to many global nomads and have found that, by and large, we all behave in similar ways. We seek out diversity wherever we are, and are attracted by people with perceived differences rather than repulsed by them. In many ways we are comfortable serving as bridges between culturally diverse groups, because we can. It's an important role and one that we're proud of.

I realize that there is one key lesson in all this. Yes, the transition between cultures was difficult, even painful. The trip back to my "home culture" was perhaps the most difficult thing I have ever done, but I wouldn't trade my experiences for anything in the world. I have talents that are valuable and meaningful. I worked hard for them. They are talents that can be put to good use if they are understood by the right people. In fact, many global nomads become educators, mediators, or professional counselors, as part of their need to provide cultural bridges.

During interviews with Peace Corps volunteers I found that, without exception, the most important thing they feel they bring home from their experiences abroad is a sense of tolerance and appreciation for cultures that are different from their own. I have to agree. I believe that Peace Corps jobs, certain overseas military assignments, multinational positions in foreign countries, and similar experiences are enormously valuable and can help bridge the cultural gaps between people and nations that stem from misunderstanding and can be so destructive. If more people, especially young people, could experience cross-cultural immersion, perhaps there would be far less violence and anger in the world. Instead of perceiving a social threat in a group of people speaking a foreign language, dressing in exotic garb, or listening to unfamiliar music, they might be curious and make an effort to understand them, perhaps even talk to them. What a concept!

Are all expatriates negatively affected by cross-cultural transition? The answer is an unequivocal *yes*, although the degree varies, depending on many factors. The personal and professional impacts often overlap and become difficult to distinguish, as the information on the following pages will illustrate. What *is* important is that the degree of negative impact, whether personal or professional, can be minimized and the positive impacts enhanced.

I wrote this book to serve as a guide for managers of overseas employees and for those employees and their families. It addresses the needs of employees who have accepted employment outside their passport country, the companies that employ them, and their family members. Living overseas is a unique experience that should not be missed, provided that the company, the employee, and the family are prepared for it. The challenges encountered by cross-cultural employees and their families, particularly those related to reentry, are daunting. Preparation for an overseas assignment should be undertaken prior to accepting the position, and all family members should take part.

This book also examines the challenges of expatriate workforce management and offers a comprehensive strategy for the difficult and complex tasks of selecting, placing, supporting, evaluating, and bringing employees and their families home. It is based on actual case studies of multinational companies and of employees who have successfully crossed the great divide between cultures. Quotes from these individuals appear throughout the book. Questions for review are included to help the reader focus on the key issues in each chapter and to generate discussion between employees and their supervisors or among family members.

Managing Cross-Cultural Transition has seven major sections. The first examines the history, growth, and role of the multinational corporation. The second discusses assessment and selection criteria for employees considering an international position. The third examines the move abroad, including preparation for it.

Part 4 looks at in-country transition, while the fifth section examines reentry. Part 6 considers the special needs of expatriate children, and the final section guides the creation of a corporate strategy for selecting, placing, evaluating, and managing an expatriate workforce.

The book discusses all phases of the acculturation process, equips individuals and companies with tools to manage the challenges discussed in each chapter, and prepares them for a rewarding time abroad and a rich and fulfilling career upon their return.

1

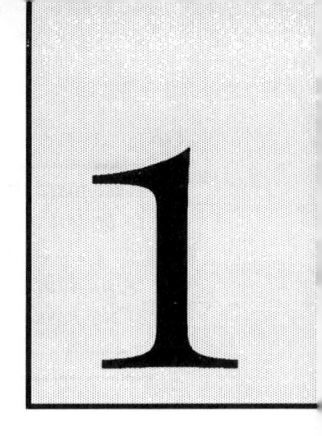

The Multinational Corporation

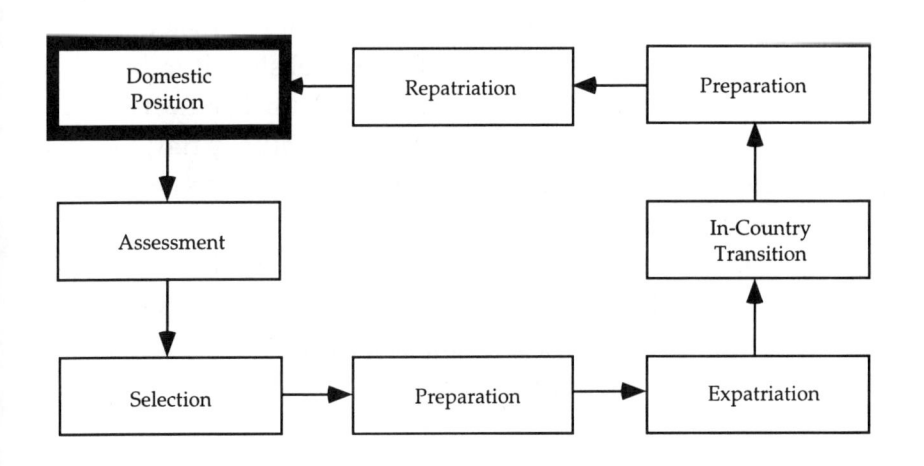

Domestic Position	←	Repatriation	←	Preparation
↓				↑
Assessment				In-Country Transition
↓				↑
Selection	→	Preparation	→	Expatriation

> *Recognize that every "out front" maneuver you make is going to be lonely. If you feel entirely comfortable, then you're not far enough ahead to do any good. That warm sense of everything going well is usually the body temperature at the center of the herd.*
>
> Anonymous sign on an office wall

The story of expatriates and multinationals began long before today's era of modern business. It started centuries ago, when adventurous explorers left their own comfortable shores and sailed off to find fame and riches in unfamiliar lands that lay beyond the horizon. Perhaps the first expatriates were Norse Vikings; there is archaeological evidence suggesting that they landed in North America long before southern European explorers did. Alternatively, they may have been Roman soldiers and administrators, posted to some remote part of the Roman empire to complete their obligatory ten years of service.

Later there were Spanish, Portuguese, French, and British colonists, sent off to establish cultural beachheads in far-flung lands. Spain launched fleet after fleet of frail sailing vessels that eventually traveled as far as the Pacific coast of what would someday become California, then on to Japan and other exotic reaches of the Far East. French and Portuguese explorers settled large tracts of Africa and South America, and colonialism made hegemony an acceptable practice in its time.

Rather than take advantage of the often well-developed cultures of the countries they occupied, many nations simply buried them under the considerable weight of their own exported culture. Not only was this process destructive, it was counterproductive to the long-term goals of the invader.

A country's cultural behaviors develop for a reason. They are always tightly connected to the souls of the people who live there, and to suppress a culture is to suppress a people. Forcefully overlaid cultures typically function well for a short period of time, but eventually the local population grows tired and begins to rebel. The rebellion may be passive and long-term, as happened in India with Gandhi, or rapid and violent, as happened in Uganda during the 1970s. It can also be reflected in economic upheaval: Witness the nationalization of the oil industry in Libya during the 1960s, and the resultant multinational exodus.

Either way, rebellion does eventually occur, and it is almost always successful. Typically some vestiges of the invading culture hang on and become assimilated into local cultural behaviors, such as language, accents, or business practices; however, they tend to be nothing more than mild spices in the cultural cooking pot.

During the post-Colonial period a new flood of expatriates headed overseas. These included members of the diplomatic corps, fledgling multinationals attempting to establish business relations overseas for the first time, and military personnel.

Their approaches were quite different from those of their predecessors.

For the most part, diplomatic and military personnel were relatively unaffected by moves overseas. Foreign Service employees were carefully coached and educated before they accepted an overseas assignment, and they usually became sensitive to the cultural mores of their hosts. Military personnel tended to live on American bases and were largely isolated from their surroundings. For the most part, they were not required to interact with the culture of the host country, and in many cases were discouraged from doing so, in order to reduce the potential for cultural conflict.

Multinational corporations, on the other hand, have every reason to interact with their hosts and become culturally sensitive. Their goal is to develop business relationships based on mutual trust, a far cry from the ethnocentric, hegemonic behavior that often preceded them. For the most part they succeed, and over the years their businesses have flourished. In fact, the world's 100 largest multinationals are so large that they would qualify for the Fortune 500 list on the basis of the value of their U.S. operations alone.

Some multinationals, however, don't succeed. International business casebooks are filled with sometimes funny, often disastrous examples of corporations that failed to do their homework prior to pursuing business in another country, only to be rebuffed by the country's government or by the would-be partner in the venture, usually for failure to take into account some minor—but critical—cultural or language-related detail. When a major fountain pen manufacturer marketed a ballpoint in Mexico, its ads were supposed to say "It won't leak in your pocket and embarrass you." However, the company mistakenly used the Spanish word *embarazar*, a seeming cognate, to mean "embarrass." As a result, the ads promised that "It won't leak in your pocket and make you pregnant."

In some cases, however, multinational corporations learn to be culturally astute. They test and select their employees for overseas assignments on the basis of their ability to adapt to the new environment, and often provide training and orientation to help them adjust to their new culture. Those employees who learn to adapt typically succeed. Those who enter a country with the belief that "it won't be good or bad, it'll just be different" usually do well and learn to roll with the cultural punches.

The typical modern multinational corporation is quite sophisticated. It is a multifaceted company that is well suited to support multiple operations both at home and abroad. It has highly capable finance and accounting departments that are well versed in dealing with multinational finance, hyperinflation, the intricacies of acceptable international accounting practices, and repatriation of funds.

What the company often lacks, however, is a well-executed plan for assessment, selection, placement, compensation, management, evaluation, repatriation, and domestic reacculturation of the expatriate employee that is integrated with the corporate business plan and creates an environment that is attractive to the employee in the long term. The issues that a typical plan addresses are discussed briefly in the following pages, and in detail throughout the remainder of the book.

Of course, the issues addressed here are not unique to the operations or employees of multinational corporations. They can be equally vexing for students studying abroad, members of the clergy, employees of volunteer organizations, journalists, and long-term travelers. In fact, those involved don't necessarily have to move abroad to be affected by cross-cultural transition: In a large country like the United States, a move from one coast to another, from the laid-back lifestyle of southern California to the northern reaches of New England, can be a profoundly powerful cross-cultural experience with its own set of long-term effects. Individuals and companies would be wise to recognize that while offshore[1] transfers are often the most difficult, in-country moves have their own daunting challenges to be faced.

Outbound

When corporations create overseas subsidiaries, they are often unaware of the business, economic, and cultural differences that employees face if they are selected for an overseas assignment. Most companies provide basic transition services for their overseas-bound employees, such as language training, a modicum of familiarization with the host culture, and a financial incentive to accept an overseas position. However, they often overlook less tangible aspects of the move that might affect the employee and their family, such as:

- whether or not to sell a home prior to departure
- what to do with pets (are they allowed in the host country?)
- whether the employee's spouse will be able to secure work in the host country
- what to do about income that is lost when one partner is transferred abroad and their working partner must quit their job
- whether the company will pay for private school for children in countries whose educational systems may not provide the equivalent of a domestic education

Unquestionably, the corporation's primary responsibility is to manage the transition of its employees and to ensure that their move abroad is as smooth and painless as possible. All too often, however, corporations forget that they may be moving a family as well, and that the family's happiness will figure prominently in the employee's success. Their transition overseas as a so-called "trailing family" is destined to be as challenging as that of the employee, and failure to prepare them appropriately can lead to social discomfort, transition difficulties, and in severe cases, failure of the employee in the assignment.

There are serious pitfalls on the outbound side that can affect employees and their families if they are not prepared for and managed properly. They don't end once the expatriates are in-country, however; there are just as many pitfalls on the inbound side.

Inbound

When expatriates return to their passport country, they are generally not prepared for the very different culture that confronts them. For example, the corporation has changed while they were away. There may be new players on the game board and new people in positions of power. And, in spite of the important role that the expatriate played while overseas, they have still been physically (and therefore psychically) removed from office activities. They are an unknown quantity and have not benefited from the "water cooler effect"—the informal sharing of information that goes on continually during day-to-day contact at the office.

Technical employees often suffer professionally as a result of the separation. When the technical employee is stationed in the third world, or in any country where the employee's own technical knowledge is significantly advanced compared to that of the local staff, the expatriate often returns home to find that his or her technical capabilities have eroded because of separation from peers, timely information sources, trade journals, schools, seminars and trade shows, and simple "office osmosis."

Because of the organizational structure of many overseas operations, expatriate managers often have far broader fiscal and managerial responsibilities than their domestic counterparts. They must make economic decisions that would require a nod from several levels of management in the domestic organization. When these people return to a stateside assignment, their responsibility level is often reduced, and they begin to feel bored and sometimes worry that they are not trusted. They go through a classic series of emotional stages: They become bored, then frustrated, then angry. Then they leave.

The expatriate changes emotionally as well. The culture in which they have lived is very different from that of the passport country. Day-to-day activities, work relationships, ethics and cultures, even weekend, evening, and vacation activities—all join forces to equip the expatriate with rich and diverse memories, behaviors, and response mechanisms that are different from those of their stateside peers. When they return home, what do they have in common with their domestic peers? How do they become reintegrated into the workplace and the general culture?

The impact on home life can also be profound. Just as the employee may have difficulty fitting in at the office, families often experience similar stresses. Faced with the demands of acculturation,[2] and perhaps not understanding what it is that makes repatriation so difficult, many families undergo a severe emotional trauma that can tear at the fabric of the family and carry over into the work environment. The combination of stresses rapidly becomes a vicious cycle.

Spouses play a major role in this equation. They often suffer from reverse culture shock as severely as the employee. Once home, the former expatriate can at least interact with other expatriates at work; the spouse may not have that luxury. At best, the impact is annoying; at worst, it can devastate a family and wreak havoc on a career.

A study released in 1971 by Gillian Purcer-Smith[3] in *Studies of International Mobility* concludes that an employee's satisfaction and success in a foreign assignment depends more than any other factor on the happiness of the spouse. By extension, the reverse is also true: If the spouse's needs are not met when the family returns home, the employee's ability to reenter the domestic workforce will be seriously compromised.

Because of the culture of the host country, income disparities, or social position, expatriates often find themselves living at social levels well above those they would be part of at home. The stateside return, therefore, can be a jarring (at best!) experience.

In many countries, standard housing is an apartment or flat downtown, and the only true "houses" are reserved for the country's wealthy. Expatriates who want to live in a private house as they would at home may find themselves suddenly elevated into lofty social realms. Homes are often quite large, and the return to a "real house" in the passport country can be a shock.

Neither the expatriate employee nor his or her family know what to expect socially when they return home. Typically, they expect to be viewed as something special, as "returning heroes." And they usually are, for the first few weeks. After the stories have been told and the newness wears off, however, the returning hero begins to look more like some kind of exotic jungle specimen than just another employee or neighbor. They dress strangely. They talk funny. And they're always bragging about "their time in Europe." These people are show-offs, plain and simple.

In point of fact, while there may be a certain amount of showing off involved, that typically isn't what's going on. After all, these people have returned from an unusual and challenging assignment, and they're proud of what they've done. They deserve a certain amount of admiration. As for social braggadocio, expatriates talk about the only things they know—namely, the experiences they collected during their time abroad.

It's no wonder that many expatriates jump at the first chance they have to change companies and return to an overseas assignment.

Statistics of Success—or Failure

In addition to the personal challenges of an overseas assignment, there are striking business impacts. Since 1970 the number of American companies with operations outside the United States has expanded dramatically. Today there are more than 3,500 true multinational corporations, and 25,000 smaller companies have overseas affiliates or branches. To staff their foreign operations, these multinational corporations rely on a cadre of willing expatriate employees, estimated to be on the order of 1,300,000 people.[4]

These employees are selected for overseas assignments for a number of reasons. In many cases they are up and coming in the corporate hierarchy and need the seasoning effects of an international assignment. Or they possess unique skills that are required for a particular task. In some companies an international assignment is simply part of the employee development strategy.

Whatever the reason for their selection, most multinationals prepare employees and their families reasonably well for international assignments. Consequently, most find the experience enriching, rewarding, and fun.

Unfortunately, things occasionally go awry when the time comes for the employee to return home. While most multinationals prepare the employee for their overseas assignment, they typically do comparatively little to prepare them for their eventual return. This transition is often so devastating that many employees leave the company that sent them overseas in the first place. Well-documented numbers bear this up: 25 percent of all expatriates resign within a year of their return; 40 percent resign within two years.[5] And where do they go? Often to the competition, where they can peddle their expertise to a company that appreciates their unique knowledge and capabilities. Or they retreat to another overseas assignment. Either way, the company—and to a large extent the employee—loses.

The reasons cited by returning expatriates for this intellectual hegira are complex yet readily understood. More than 35 percent of overseas employees conclude that there is no belief within their company that the overseas experience is enriching or that it makes for a better employee.[6] At best, the company is viewed as indifferent.

An equally disturbing statistic indicates that 65 percent of expatriate employees are not guaranteed a job upon their return.[7] This is particularly disconcerting to expatriates, who feel empowered and capable as a result of their overseas experience, yet frustrated by the fact that physical separation from headquarters has kept them out of the job loop. When they *do* return to the domestic organization, more than half of them express frustration and anger because their hard-earned, unique, and powerful skills are not used. In fact, although 65 percent of employees preparing to go overseas believe that the experience will be rewarding and career-enhancing, 77 percent conclude after they have returned to their passport country that the impact on their career has been profoundly negative.[8]

Finally, only 25 percent of returning expatriates receive any form of repatriation counseling to prepare them for reentry.[9] Many companies take the stance that their employees were adequately prepared to enter a foreign culture prior to shipping out; why should they need any form of counseling when they come home? After all, this is where they came from.

In fact, many companies treat repatriation as a form of rescue: They are pulling the employee out of a hostile environment and bringing them home, when in fact the reverse is more accurate. The foreign post is now home; the passport country is just another foreign assignment. Thus, this perspective on the part of the corporation is not only wrong but also potentially destructive.

Global human resources managers estimate that the loaded cost[10] of an expatriate employee is between four and five times the employee's annual salary. Eric Campbell, director of global human resources for Avon Products, Inc., estimates from his experience that the average fully loaded expense is roughly a quarter of a million dollars a year—provided that the employee is not in a high-cost area such as London, Hong Kong, Geneva, or Paris, where costs are considerably higher.[11] Several recent surveys indicate that annual living expenses alone (food, clothing, housing, medical care, etc.) for a couple without children in these higher-cost areas exceed $150,000. One study clearly illustrated how an employee who earns an $80,000 annual salary can easily become a $250,000-per-year employee.

Because of the growth of lucrative international markets and evolving trade agreements such as the European Community, the General Agreement on Tariffs and Trade/World Trade Organization, and the North American Free Trade Agreement, domestic corporations are scrambling to become multinationals. In fact, multinational corporations (MNCs) are more the rule than the exception today. It costs these corporations millions of dollars to educate and place a multinational workforce in-country. After several years abroad, those people amass a valuable set of skills and cultural sensitivities that are, quite literally, priceless. They can't be taught: they must be learned through a form of subconscious, cultural osmosis.

The shrewd corporation, therefore, must take aggressive steps to create a program that recognizes international employees as valuable assets, not liabilities. It must choose them carefully for overseas assignments, place them correctly, and care for them properly during their sojourn abroad. When the time comes, the company has the responsibility to repatriate them emotionally, culturally, and professionally, help their families survive the difficult transition of reentry, and place them in jobs that are challenging and rewarding and that take advantage of their unique skills.

Alternatively, the company can place the employee in an overseas assignment as routinely as they transfer a person domestically, repatriate them anonymously and without fanfare, ignore the cultural, social, and professional impact on the employee and their family, place them in a job that bores, frustrates, and angers them, and then watch them leave and join a competing firm within a year.

The company that understands the transition that a returning expatriate must go through to rejoin the domestic workforce can immediately take advantage of that person's skills and eliminate much of the culture shock that the employee experiences. At the same time, the employee who can anticipate the changes that are in store can minimize the impact on themselves and on their immediate family. Most important, by doing these things the company retains a valuable employee and the employee keeps a long-term, rewarding job. Everyone wins.

The "globalization" of the modern corporation is under way. The number of corporate employees who work outside their home country is rising, and those numbers will *continue* to grow as trade barriers fall away, political restrictions such as CoCOM[12] become archaic and unnecessary, and economic disparities between nations are reduced. Corporations that understand the special needs of their expatriate workers and that take steps to satisfy those needs will be ahead of the pack, and will realize significant rewards for their efforts.

Summary

As corporations evolve into sophisticated global organizations, they learn to be culturally astute, geocentric rather than ethnocentric, and linguistically, geographically, and economically agile. They select and place a workforce that manages their overseas subsidiaries, and they are largely successful in their international ventures. To remain successful and to ensure the long-term satisfaction, high performance, and employment of staff members, they must put into place a program that is geared toward management of the expatriate employee before, during, and after the overseas assignment.

Questions for Review

1. What were the forces that caused postcolonial expatriates to approach overseas markets with a greater focus on and sensitivity to the host culture?

2. Why are multinational corporations becoming more common? Will this trend continue?

3. Why are MNCs often not attuned to the issues associated with selecting, creating, and placing a multinational workforce?

4. Comment on the following statement: "The best way to approach life in a new cultural environment is to recognize that it won't be good or bad, simply different."

5. What are some of the critical factors that corporations and employees must consider during the outbound phase of an international assignment? What about the inbound phase?

6. It is just as critical to care for the needs of the expatriate employee's family as it is to care for those of the employee. Explain.

Notes

1. "Offshore" organizations refer to the overseas subsidiaries of domestic corporations. They are physically located in other countries, often on different continents; hence the use of the term.

2. The process of adjusting to life in a new culture.

3. Gillian Purcer-Smith, *Studies of International Mobility* (New York: National Foreign Trade Council, 1971).

4. Based on IRS filed tax return information and data from Bureau of Economic Analysis, U.S. Department of Commerce. This number does not include military personnel, nor does it include family members.

5. From Eric Raimy, "Repat Roulette," *Human Resource Executive,* November 1994, pp. 51–54.

6. *Ibid.*

7. *Ibid.* This assumes, of course, that the employment contract did not explicitly state that there would be no job waiting when their overseas assignment was complete.

8. *Ibid.*

9. *Ibid.*

10. The "loaded cost" of an employee represents the actual cost of employment. It includes not only the employee's

salary but also retirement benefits, medical insurance, corporate savings plans, and in the case of overseas employees, the additional costs to maintain them and their family in-country.

11. *Ibid.*

12. Coordinating Committee on Export Controls, a government organization charged with controlling the export of certain types of products.

2

Employee Assessment and Selection

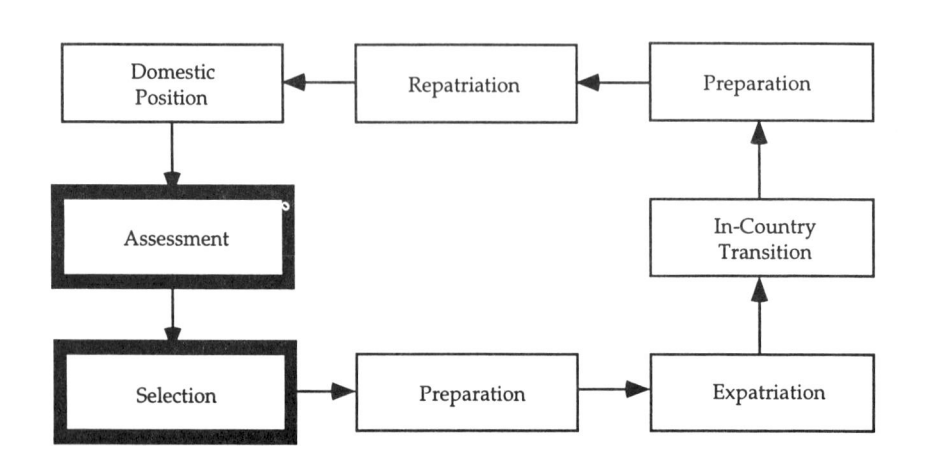

```
Domestic  ← Repatriation  ← Preparation
Position                          ↑
   ↓                         In-Country
**Assessment**               Transition
   ↓                              ↑
**Selection** → Preparation → Expatriation
```

> "It has always seemed strange to me," said Doc. "The things we admire in men, kindness and generosity, openness, honesty, understanding and feeling, are the concomitants of failure in our system. And those traits we detest, sharpness, greed, acquisitiveness, egotism and self-interest, are the traits of success. And while men admire the quality of the first they love the produce of the second."
>
> John Steinbeck, *Cannery Row*

Employees are selected for international assignments for a variety of reasons—often because they possess a specific skill that is required in the host country but not available locally, or because an international assignment is required for employees who have been identified for higher management positions within the corporation—often called "getting their ticket punched."

An international assignment is exciting, gratifying, and more than a little frightening for both the employee and their family. An employee who has been selected for an overseas assignment must go into the position with both eyes open and all questions answered.

Successful multinational companies have clearly defined, well-written, well-defended, and accessible policies that support their rationale for sending employees overseas. Unfortunately, this practice is not universal. In fact, a study conducted jointly by the National Foreign Trade Council and SRI[1] found that while 62 percent of the employees interviewed believed that their companies have a clearly defined strategy for doing business abroad, only 50 percent of them felt that the strategy was properly communicated.

The rationale for sending an employee overseas should align closely with organizational structure and corporate operating philosophy. In some cases, however, because of naive or inexperienced management, international transfers are undertaken as lightly as intracountry transfers, with little understanding of the profound differences between the two. One study found that 65 percent of the members of one group of soon-to-be expatriates expressed a belief that the international experience would have a positive impact on their career. Upon their return, 77 percent of the same group indicated that the impact was in fact negative.[2]

The prospective expatriate should ensure that the corporation's reasons for sending them overseas are in keeping with their own reasons for going:

> I came home from Riyadh feeling pretty special. I learned a second language, and knew how to do business in a different culture. But when I finally came home, it seemed as if nobody knew who I was, and just as bad, I didn't know much about what they were doing. I felt like Rip Van Winkle.

In addition to the tangible, business-specific reasons for sending an employee overseas, there are intangible factors that must be assessed as part of the selection process. Besides exceptional work performance, good management skills, and proper work ethics, the potential expatriate employee must be culturally flexible and unbiased, and able to adapt to a wide range of environments in both personal and professional situations. Obviously, language skills and prior experience carry considerable weight, although they are less critical than flexibility in the long run. Languages can be learned, and experience comes from—well, experience. (During the seventh century, St. Augustine observed that "the reward of patience is patience.")

These intangible qualities include the following:

- Personality traits that would be conducive to success in a transnational work environment: open-mindedness, flexibility, tolerance, trust, cross-cultural respect, and the like.

- The perceived ability of the employee's family to successfully adapt to the cross-cultural environment.

- Biases or attitudes toward other cultures.

- Prior experience abroad or language ability.

- Unique needs or circumstances, such as specialized schooling; physical and emotional health of family members; strength of the relationship between the employee and spouse; job availability for the spouse, if applicable.

Employee Selection

The criteria used to select employees for overseas positions are broader than those used for a domestic position. In addition to technical or managerial capability, work ethics, and ambition, the employee (and his or her family) must be assessed on the basis of other, less tangible or "soft" factors as well. For example, an employee who has received kudos for aggressive selling in the U.S. market will likely offend customers with this behavior in Latin America, the Middle East, or the Pacific Rim. Criteria such as general interpersonal skills, reasonable self-assertion, and confidence are important indicators of an employee's suitability for cross-cultural success.

Line Management versus HR

Both line management[3] requirements and human resources concerns must be considered and balanced during the employee selection process. The line organization's principal concern is to assess and select employees who exhibit the best technical skills required for the overseas position. Human Resources (HR), on the other hand, is concerned more about employee selection, compensation, career guidance, relocation, and performance evaluation. In fact, a common complaint in some companies is that HR organizations, in an attempt to properly manage all of these disparate functions, parcel them out to different groups that do not communicate with one another as well as they should. In point of fact, these concerns are equally important and must be jointly managed. Success rates vary; when employees in an NFTC/SRI study were asked about their own companies' ability to balance these forces, they made the following observations:

- Ninety-four percent of the employees interviewed said that their companies hold line management responsible for selection of candidates, and 76 percent said that Human Resources interviews candidates as well. Fifty-six percent said that line managers make final selection decisions based on their own judgment, and that HR input into that process has virtually no impact at all, in spite of exhaustive examination by HR of each candidate's work history and capabilities.

- Fifty percent of the respondents felt that their companies had successfully identified the unique success factors for overseas employees.

- Thirty-two percent indicated that their personnel planning and international employee movement strategies are linked to identified international competencies.

- Only 25 percent maintain a "talent inventory" to be used for selection and placement of personnel.

According to Jerry Hanley, who retired from AT&T as a senior executive and who at one time "had the entire world reporting to him" (he and his wife were often referred to as the patron saints of expatriates at AT&T), human resources and line management organizations are equally important, with some significant caveats.

> HR must become more of an activist organization, selling the gospel to line managers and expatriate employees alike. Line management, on the other hand, has a responsibility to the corporation to ensure that the job gets done, regardless of where it is and who's doing it. They must therefore *never* delegate or relegate their responsibilities: a balance between the two must be maintained.

The corporate business plan, personnel development strategies, line management concerns, and human resources issues must all feed into the international employee assessment strategy if it is to succeed. Some corporations create global human resources organizations that provide a functional liaison between the domestic and international organizations. They also serve as an interface between human resources and line management during both the initial selection process and the repatriation and domestic placement period.

Employee Factors

The *employee's* reasons for going overseas are equally important. Is this strictly a career move on their part, or are there personal reasons for such a dramatic change? Career advancement is one of the more common reasons cited, but others include a desire to change a lifestyle that is boring or unchallenging, a need for enhanced income, or the (usually wrong) perception that a radical change in lifestyle will save a troubled relationship.

Spouse Concerns

It is also critical to consider the spouse's position during this part of the assessment process. One study[4] of 2,000 employees from multinational corporations concluded that the spouse's satisfaction ranks as the single most decisive factor in the employee's successful adjustment to the job. While employees are transferred abroad for a variety of career-related reasons, spouses are transferred abroad because of an obligation to their partners:

> We can laugh about it now, but at the time, it wasn't very funny. The position in Saudi [Arabia] was important to my husband's career and to him personally—I knew it meant a lot to him. So even though I was scared about moving to such a culturally different place, I never said anything to anybody. I just went along, and while I liked where we lived, it took me a long time to reach that point. I really resented the fact that no one ever asked me what I thought.

More than ever before, dual-career couples are the norm rather than the exception. According to

U.S. Department of Labor statistics, 80 percent of all domestic marriages will involve dual careers by the year 2000. A Windham International/National Foreign Trade Council study conducted in 1994 found that 45 percent of all expatriate assignments involved a spouse who was employed prior to moving abroad, and 88 percent of all participants in the survey felt that spouse career issues will soon become a major contributing factor in the international career decision process.

Because of the growth of dual-career families, companies are faced with a new set of challenges. The international marketplace is competitive and requires highly skilled employees. Employees who are offered international assignments are faced with the very real problem that if they are married and have a working spouse, they will likely lose the spouse's income if the family moves abroad. If it is not addressed by the corporation, this factor may cause some of the best candidates to remove themselves from consideration for international positions, a challenge that most companies cannot afford.

Companies have crafted a variety of solutions to this problem, although few of them result in full compensation. Some offer "placement services" in cooperation with other multinationals to help spouses find work while abroad; some employ the spouse in the overseas location during the assignment, using a variety of compensation models; others create income replacement programs that attempt to replace some agreed-upon percentage of the spouse's income. Financial compensation, while a crucial consideration, is one of many.

The spouse's successful transition is a critical factor, because theirs is the most difficult transition of all. When an employee is transferred abroad, all family members give up friends and social structures. The employee, however, quickly becomes part of a peer-level social structure at work, thus minimizing interruptions in continuity. Children enter school and quickly create new social structures for themselves among their peers, thus suffering comparatively little from the shock of transition. Spouses, however, must endure considerably more upheaval. While they lose the support of their own domestic social structure, they are also usually forced to interact most closely (and soonest) with the local culture:

> When we arrived in Spain, my husband immediately got involved in his work and my kids enrolled in school. In less than a week, I found myself home alone, with no friends, almost no knowledge of the local culture, and no idea how or where to shop. I was completely lost. And on top of that, I now had a live-in maid and gardeners to deal with who spoke no English. And the worst part, besides the fact that I had nobody to go to for help, was that my husband and my kids didn't understand what I was dealing with. It was really, really hard.

Because the expatriate worker travels and must often devote inordinately long hours to work, the spouse is forced to take on a more demanding domestic role. This can become an untenable situation, because in addition to managing the household and taking care of the children single-handedly, spouses still have to deal with their own cultural transition to the new country and lifestyle.

The added pressure can place enormous strains on a relationship. The employee, after all, is deeply involved in work and surrounded by professional peers, which together provide support and camaraderie. Most companies pay a great deal of attention to the physical preparation of the employee and logistics of an offshore move, somewhat less attention to the cultural transition skills that will be required, such as acculturation and language training, and almost no time at all to the spouse's needs:

> My company took care of everything to get us over there. They managed the movers, helped us rent our house, paid for French lessons, even helped us register our kids in the school. Once we got to Kinshasa, though, it didn't take long for us to realize that a big piece had been left out of our orientation. My wife knew *nothing* about living in Africa, in spite of what we had been taught about the culture and language before we left. Thank God for the other expat wives over there; they rescued her, and helped her get a handle on things during the first few weeks. They were great, but it's something the company should have done.

Health

The employee's ability to cope with life abroad is a critical assessment factor. Are there any preexisting health or lifestyle conditions that could predispose the employee or their family to difficulties while overseas? Is there an indication or history of alcohol or substance abuse? If so, the employee must be carefully interviewed and the condition frankly discussed. Substance abuse, however minor, is often indicative of inability to manage stress properly, and stress can be chronic in overseas assignments:

> When I sent Jack to our office in Brussels, I did so because he was *without question* the best person for the job. He was the most experienced candidate, knew the product better than anybody, and had spent a lot of time with the Belgians who came over to work with us on product development. They got along well, and I knew it would be a good fit. What I *also* knew was that he had a pretty serious drinking problem, but because he had always been able to keep it under control, I didn't consider it a serious concern. Well, I was wrong: between the stress of the job, the travel, and the additional family stress from being in a new place, his drinking went completely out of control and we ended up having to bring him (and eventually, his family) home prematurely. It cost us a lot of money, but it wasn't Jack's fault—it was mine. I should have paid better attention.

The availability of specialized products may be quite different in the host country than in the home country. Unique health care products, foods, medications, and schooling for a child with special needs may not be as available as they are at home. These factors, therefore, must be considered during the selection process:

> The biggest concern we had when we moved [to Italy] was that our daughter is highly allergic to certain food additives. In England, we have access to a wide variety of natural foods that are made without any additives, but we weren't sure if they would be available when we got to Milan. So before we could make a decision about whether to accept the job, we had to make sure that we would be able to find specialty foods there. It turned out not to be a problem, but it could have been.

Age and Maturity

An employee's age can be a decisive factor during the selection process, not so much because of years, but because of professional and personal maturity, social status, and stability. While younger families often accept the major change of an international move more easily than older, more established families, the financial and interpersonal stability of a young family's relationship must be assessed early on.

> Bob had all the "right stuff" for the job in London—at least it seemed that way. He graduated at the top of his MBA class, was a good manager, and had been with the company for about three years, long enough to have a sense of the corporate culture. What he

didn't have was financial stability. He was only a few years out of school, and while he had all the right business accomplishments, we never looked into the personal stuff because we always felt that it was "none of our business." The problem is that there are lots of times overseas when you need ready access to cash, for entertaining and the like. It's all reimbursable, but when you need it, you need it *now.* Well, he didn't have it, and it developed into a somewhat embarrassing situation for him.

The things that get you are more often than not the little ones. Don't be afraid to ask: better to find out now than to wait and let it become a long-distance issue.

Other Pitfalls

It is not unusual for certain individuals to feel that an enforced change of lifestyle, such as an international move, can resuscitate a failing relationship. Nothing could be further from the truth. The typical expatriate employee often works unreasonably long hours, travels a great deal, and experiences inordinate amounts of work-related stress. The chances that these additional factors will improve a difficult marriage are exceedingly slim. The chances that an employee experiencing marital difficulties will be able to devote themselves fully to the job is equally slim. Careful assessment and frank discussion are recommended if there are indications of problems in the relationship.

> When I think about it, I'm pretty sure that we knew that the move [to Kuala Lumpur] wasn't a good idea. We didn't want to hear that, though. All we knew was that we were having problems, and we thought that the new environment would be good for us, like a breath of fresh air. Of course, now we know that all it did was accelerate the inevitable. Tom was gone most of the time, and I was stuck in a country where I didn't know the language, had no friends, and barely knew anything about the culture. It was awful. I ended up leaving him and going back to the UK. I'm sure we would have eventually split up anyway, but the added pressure that came from living where we did just made it happen a lot faster.

Finally, prior international experience and familiarity with the host country's primary language are valuable selection criteria.

Some multinational corporations use the international assignment as a managerial proving ground. Employees who are being groomed for upper management are often thrown into challenging positions so that senior staff can assess their ability to handle such a position. These are often overseas, because there is a valid perception that the company, and therefore its employees, must be able to operate effectively in a multinational environment to succeed. The number of international assignments therefore is on the rise.

In a joint study conducted in 1995 by Windham International and the National Foreign

Trade Council,[5] employees of 138 multinational corporations doing business in a wide range of countries responded to a battery of questions about international relocation. In Figure 2-1, shown on page 50, note that family adjustment ranks highest at 42 percent, with lifestyle issues a distant second at 24 percent, followed by expatriate work adjustment, wrong candidate, performance, other opportunity, business reasons, and repatriation issues.

A failed assignment, regardless of the cause, is an expensive proposition. Estimates of the cost to replace an expatriate employee and their family range from $250,000 to more than a million dollars, but the actual cost is far higher when emotional impact, domestic job placement, and transition time for the replacement employee are factored in. While careful employee evaluation and selection are crucially important, spouses and families must be counseled, advised, and assessed. It is critical for the corporation to consider these factors reasonably and realistically, and to discuss them with the employee and their family during the initial stages of the selection process. Failure to do so can be costly, both for the employee and for the corporation. After all, transition training, including proper employee selection, is far cheaper than losing even a single employee owing to poor assessment and selection practices. As one global human resources director observed: "All companies pay for assessment and selection programs. They simply pay a lot more for the ones they don't implement."

Reasons for Assignment Failure

Category	Value
Family Adjustment	~40
Lifestyle Issues	~23
Expatriate Work Adjustment	~18
Wrong Candidate	~13
Performance	~10
Other Opportunity	~6
Business Reasons	~5
Repatriation Issues	~3

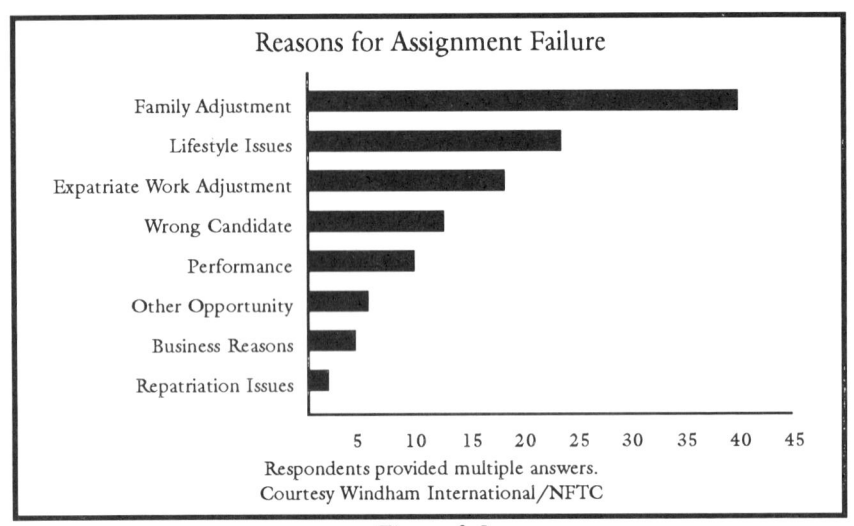

Respondents provided multiple answers.
Courtesy Windham International/NFTC

Figure 2-1

Some companies have developed questionnaires for employees and their families to complete prior to entering the selection process for an international assignment. They require the employee, their spouse, and any older children who will be affected by an overseas move to respond to a series of questions during the early stages of selection. These questionnaires are carefully designed to help potential expatriates consider all aspects of an international move and to recognize that there are serious considerations involved in taking on an overseas assignment.

Once all family members have completed the forms, discussed their answers, and determined that they are still interested in an overseas post, they begin a managerial evaluation process that assesses the employee's technical and managerial skills, which satisfy the needs of line management, and their interpersonal and cross-cultural skills, which satisfy the concerns of Human Resources. The evaluation should also assess the family's readiness for an overseas assignment.

An example is shown on the following pages.

A PREASSESSMENT EXERCISE

The exercise that follows is based on assessment tools used by many multinational corporations. It is designed to help potential expatriate employees and their families assess their readiness for an overseas assignment.

The exercise consists of five sections. The first three present a series of questions for each family member to answer independently. These are designed to help them assess what the overseas assignment will mean to them. The fourth section is a family synthesis exercise, in which family members compare their answers and discuss them; and the final section is a decision exercise.

Try to consider all questions from both positive and negative points of view and answer them accordingly, taking into account both viewpoints.

Employee Assessment Exercise

Please set aside enough time to answer the following questions fully—perhaps an hour. Answer all questions as honestly, completely, and candidly as you can.

What will an overseas assignment mean for my career path? Will there be a downside to leaving my present job?

In what way will an overseas assignment affect my personal growth? Do I perceive a downside?

In what ways will an overseas assignment affect my career development, both positively and negatively?

Do I understand all the financial considerations that might be involved in taking on an overseas assignment?

How might an overseas move affect my job security, employability, and retirement benefits?

Do the travel and adventure associated with an overseas lifestyle appeal to me?

Will an overseas assignment bring me prestige in the company and in my personal life?

Are there any health concerns that I should consider before taking on an overseas assignment?

Will a move abroad affect any hobbies, activities, or outside interests that are important to me?

Does the prospect of selling my home or renting it to strangers bother me?

Does the prospect of storing my valuables and personal effects bother me?

How do I feel about leaving behind friends, in-laws, grandparents, churches, social organizations?

How do I feel about leaving the location and climate where I currently live?

Am I willing to learn a new language?

Spouse Assessment Exercise

Please set aside enough time to answer the following questions fully—perhaps an hour. Answer all questions as honestly, completely, and candidly as you can.

What will an overseas assignment mean for my own career path? Is it worth it to me and to my family to leave my *own* job so that my spouse can accept an overseas assignment (if applicable)?

In what way will an overseas assignment affect my personal growth? Do I perceive a downside?

In what ways will an overseas assignment affect my own career development, both positively and negatively? What if there are no jobs for me in the host country?

Do I understand all the financial considerations that might be involved in taking on an overseas assignment?

How might an overseas move affect my job security, employability, and retirement benefits?

Do the travel and adventure associated with an overseas lifestyle appeal to me?

Will an overseas assignment bring me prestige?

Are there any health concerns that I should consider before moving overseas?

Will a move abroad affect any hobbies, activities, or outside interests that are important to me?

Does the prospect of selling my home or renting it to strangers bother me?

Does the prospect of storing my valuables and personal effects bother me?

How do I feel about leaving behind friends, in-laws, grandparents, churches, social organizations?

How do I feel about leaving the location and climate where I currently live?

Am I willing to learn a new language?

Child Assessment Exercise (Assisted)

Older children: Please set aside enough time to answer the following questions fully—perhaps an hour. Answer all questions as honestly, completely, and candidly as you can.

Parents should help their younger children answer the following questions. To get the maximum benefit from the exercise, take care that you do not lead them to answers; let them contribute their own unassisted thoughts.

What does it mean to me to move overseas?

In what way will an overseas assignment be good for me? Does it scare me?

How do I feel about leaving behind friends, loved ones, my school, and my social life?

Do the travel and adventure associated with an overseas lifestyle appeal to me?

Will an overseas assignment bring me prestige?

Will a move abroad affect any hobbies, activities, or outside interests that are important to me?

Does the prospect of storing my valuables and personal effects bother me?

How do I feel about leaving behind friends, in-laws, grandparents, churches, social organizations?

How do I feel about leaving the location and climate where I currently live?

Am I willing to learn a new language?

Synthesis

Have each family member review their answers to the preassessment questions. Then, as a family, discuss the answers to each question. Every family member should be given the opportunity to express their answers, concerns, and fears without interruption or argument. Keep in mind that an overseas move affects all family members, so all should have an equal opportunity to talk.

Once everyone has had an opportunity to share their answers, use the following questions to further guide the discussion. As before, everyone should be given equal opportunity to speak.

Are there any places we would not go? Why?

Are there any places we would really like to go if given a choice? Why?

How long would we be willing to live outside our passport country?

What is the best part of accepting an overseas assignment?

What is the worst part of accepting an overseas assignment?

Are we flexible enough to be able to start a new life in a new country, understanding that many things will be very different from life at home?

Making an Informed Decision

When everyone in the family has had an opportunity to talk and all questions have been answered, there should be enough information at hand to facilitate a decision about whether to pursue an overseas assignment. This exercise provides a framework for discussing the key issues associated with a move overseas.

If questions remain at the end of the exercise, the employee should seek answers to them before proceeding with a decision.

When the family has completed the exercise, discussed concerns about the move, and decided whether to proceed, the company can use the information obtained from it as a guideline for further discussions with the employee.

Summary

The living conditions and cultural environment during an overseas assignment, regardless of venue, will be dramatically different for the expatriate family. The ability to accept and adapt to a new lifestyle can be a pivotal success factor for both the employee and the family. If the family encounters adjustment difficulties, the employee will have to become involved, and work performance may suffer. Careful planning on the part of both the employee and the company can help reduce the difficulties of expatriation and assimilation.

It is important that personal factors such as maturity, family stability, and health be discussed candidly and sensitively with the employee early in the selection process. Failure to do so can have devastating results for both the employee and the company.

Questions for Review

1. List as many reasons as you can why employees are selected by corporate management for overseas positions.

2. Why would a domestic corporation not view an overseas assignment as important?

3. List several reasons why the business plan for an overseas organization will differ from that of its domestic counterpart.

4. On the basis of the answer to the preceding question, how is employee selection affected?

5. During employee selection for an overseas position, what qualities are more important: work performance and management skills, or intangible issues such as language ability, cultural awareness, and family stability? How should managers rank these selection criteria?

6. Why do line managers and Human Resources departments occasionally clash over employee selection criteria? How can these differences be ameliorated?

7. When employees are transferred abroad, the loss of the spouse's income is a very real concern for many employees. How should corporations address this issue? Can it be dealt with effectively?

8. Why is the spouse's transition sometimes considered to be more challenging than that of the employee?

9. How might the corporation facilitate the spouse's transition? Should it attempt to do so?

Notes

1. National Foreign Trade Council and SRI (Selection Research International), *International Sourcing and Selection Practices*. New York, September 1995.

2. Eric Raimy, "Rapat Roulette," *Human Resource Executive*, November 1994.

3. "Line management" refers to the organization that is managerially responsible for the people performing a task and for the task itself. For example, many corporations locate manufacturing facilities in other countries because of the need to be near the market, to take advantage of lower labor prices, and other considerations. The staff responsible for the day-to-day operation of the plant, management of employees, and task and project guidance are considered to be line management.

4. Gillian Purcer-Smith, *Studies of International Mobility in IBM World Trade Corporation*. New York: National Foreign Trade Council, 1971.

5. Windham International and the National Foreign Trade Council (NFTC), *Global Relocation Trends 1995 Survey Report*. New York, December 1995.

Preparation and Expatriation

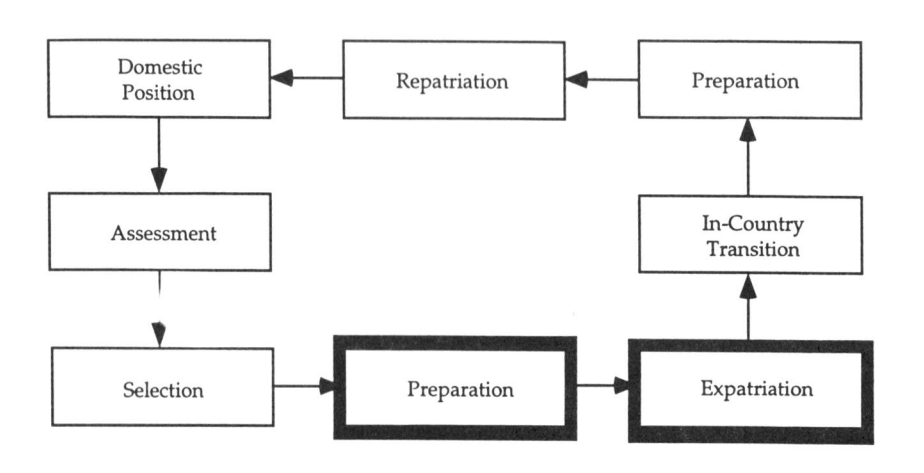

Domestic Position	←	Repatriation	←	Preparation
Assessment				In-Country Transition
Selection	→	**Preparation**	→	**Expatriation**

> *What to Take: Let your trunk, if you have to buy one, be of moderate size and of the strongest make. Test it by throwing it from the top of a three-storied house; if you pick it up uninjured, it will do to go to Kansas. Not otherwise.*
>
> James Redpath and Richard Hinton,
> *Handbook to Kansas Territory (1859)*

The overall expatriate experience consists of three major phases: *expatriation,* which comprises selection, predeparture orientation, and the actual expatriation process; *in-country transition,* which consists of orientation, a settling-in period, and eventually, preparation for reentry; and finally *repatriation,* which includes prereturn orientation, physical repatriation, and domestic orientation.

Predeparture Orientation

When the employee selection process is complete, the corporation should prepare the employee to operate within unfamiliar social and business cultures. In some companies, training programs have been designed that prepare the employee and their family for successful assimilation into the host country's culture. These programs are necessarily based on a rich understanding of both the source culture and the culture of the host country.

> One thing we did was to get a bunch of French money—all the different denominations, both bills

and coins—and spent a lot of time just playing with the values, getting used to them, converting back and forth from francs to dollars, and so on. It really helped us to get accustomed to the money, which is so important.

Once the employee has been selected for an overseas post, they and their family should prepare for the upcoming transition. There is a well-defined process, known to sociologists, that plots the stages an individual or family goes through during the expatriation/repatriation process. This model, known as the W-curve hypothesis model,[1] is shown below. It, or some form of it, can be used to help employees and their families who are contemplating a move abroad understand what they will go through.

The model charts the predictable stages of initial entry shock, settling in (acculturation, awareness, acceptance), and readjustment and adaptation following the return home.

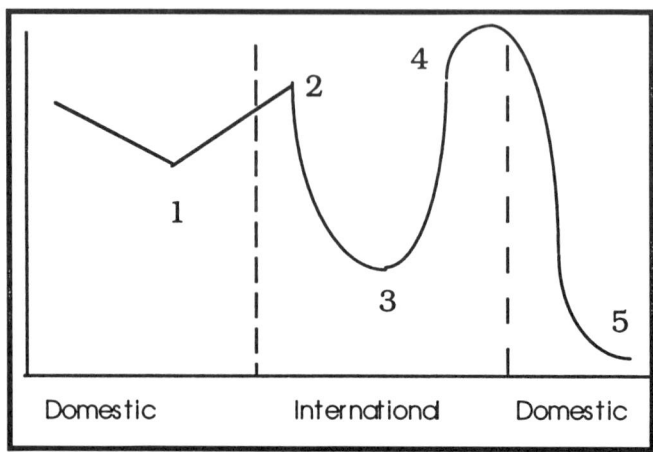

Figure 3-1: The W-Curve

Prior to departure for an overseas assignment, employees often feel reasonably comfortable in their jobs, although most admit that things could perhaps be better (1). When they accept the new position, there is a sharp rise in anxiety as culture shock hits (2), but it quickly abates as acculturation, awareness, and acceptance begin to take hold (3).

When the employee and their family return home, there is another predictable spike in anxiety as they reenter (4); as before, adjustment and adaptation eventually take place (5).

Corporate human resources managers can use the model as a discussion tool to prepare employees for their new life. Ideally, human resources staff who are responsible for expatriate personnel and their well-being should be former expatriates themselves. If they are to make decisions that are in the expatriate's best interests, they should have a first-hand understanding of what the expatriate lifestyle is like. If this is not possible, then HR should employ an "advisory council" of former expatriates to help with the management of current expatriates.

Key Eakin[2] describes the assimilation phenomenon as a five-stage process: *initial euphoria,* during which the expatriate is excited by the prospect of living in a new country and culture; *irritability,* when the newness begins to fade and reality starts to creep in; *hostility,* as the expatriate starts to miss home; *gradual adjustment,* during which the expatriate's level of comfort with the language and the culture improve to functional levels; and finally, *adaptation and acceptance.*

When expatriates leave their home country, the transition, while exciting, is often emotional and painful. They must relinquish long-standing relationships and support structures with friends and family members, and attempt to reestablish them in a foreign country. This process inevitably leads to feelings of separation, personal loss, and denial.

In addition, the new lifestyle itself is different from the one left behind. The family now lives in a foreign country under the strictures of an unfamiliar culture. The language is new and strange, the social structure—even that of the expatriate community—peculiar.

The family structure itself may change. In some overseas situations it is customary to employ servants—maids, nannies, butlers, chauffeurs—who rapidly become an integral part of the "extended family." Also, family members often become emotionally closer and more dependent on each other during an overseas assignment because of the additional unfamiliar pressures. This can sometimes create problems for teens, because separation anxiety can be exacerbated when they leave for college or move out on their own:

> When I left Madrid for college I was excited, but once I got there, I felt completely and totally lost. I didn't know anybody, I couldn't fit in with any of the groups there, and I really missed my family. It took me a long time to get over that—much longer than any of my friends.

> It's funny—I missed my family a lot, but the person I really missed was Marta [the family's live-in maid]. She and I had grown close in the three years that she lived with us, and it was really hard for me to get over the fact that she wasn't there. I guess I mentally prepared myself for the fact that I would miss my parents and sister, but for some reason I never considered my relationship with Marta. That really cost me.

Preparation and Counseling

In addition to human resources personnel, some multinational corporations use professional counselors to help prepare soon-to-be expatriates for their time abroad. According to an NFTC/SRI report, however, only 10 percent of the companies surveyed provide assessment training to their interviewers that is specifically oriented toward the selection of overseas employees. In fact, 29 percent said that their interviewers receive no evaluation training at all. Sixty-five percent of the interviewed participants said that their interviewers receive a standard domestic-centered assessment training program, while 15 percent of the companies rely on the skills of an outside consultant to train their internal interviewers.

It is normal to be apprehensive, even frightened, prior to departure, and professional counseling can help ease this burden. Families should be encouraged to discuss their concerns, fears, and apprehensions with counselors or human resources staff.

In addition, many companies help prepare the employee and their family by arranging "immersion time" with other employees and their families who have lived overseas. This allows the employee to ask questions about work-related issues, the spouses to share their concerns and recommendations, and the children to ask their peers about school, entertainment, and the local social scene.

Compensation details, already covered by this time, should be reviewed prior to departure. Employees should be counseled about the disparities that will exist between domestic and overseas compensation packages. If professional financial advisors are available, they should be used to help the employee and their family create a plan and operate within a financial structure that will not only support them while abroad, but address a long-term savings and investment strategy for their eventual return.

The Mentor

The appointment of a mentor for the expatriate employee can be an extremely effective practice. This person, often (but not always) the employee's stateside superior, is responsible for ensuring that the employee stationed overseas experiences as painless a transition as possible, and has an intact corporate lifeline that will keep them "in the corporate cultural loop" during their time abroad. The mentor is also responsible for guiding the repatriation of the employee and their family when the time comes for their return:

I didn't really understand what I was being asked to do when I was appointed to be Candace's mentor. In fact, I didn't realize how important my role was until she got to London, got settled in, and started bombarding me with requests for information. I had to do a lot of hand-holding during that time, and while it eventually leveled off, it never really went away, because there were always new things to prepare her for. I have now mentored four different employees during their time abroad, and each time, the pattern is exactly the same.

The Mentor's Responsibilities

There are several things that the mentor can do to ease both outbound and inbound transitions. The most important are to recognize the profound impact that an overseas assignment can have; to be sensitive to it; and to adequately prepare the employee and their family for it. Ideally, this process begins before the employee leaves their passport country. At that time the mentor should have already been thinking about the long-term responsibility to the departing employee and the need to provide support and assistance during the major phases of an international assignment: expatriation, in-country transition, and repatriation.

> I pretty much felt that once they were over there for a while, this "mentor stuff" would sort of fade away. I know better now, but back then, I thought that once the initial shock of living in a different

country went away, it would be easy from there on. Little did I know that that was just the beginning!

Two major components of the mentor's job are to ensure that the employee is kept apprised of goings-on within the domestic company, and that they are kept aware of future job prospects and other issues that concern their professional disposition following repatriation:

> Once I got my feet on the ground in Milan and felt comfortable in the job, I began to wonder about the future. I mean, there I was, thousands of miles from home, living in this gorgeous city in Europe with a chauffeur, a maid, and a villa, and I was thinking about Ohio. Sooner or later, this assignment would end and I'd have to go back—then what? It didn't take long for me to begin to feel sort of isolated over there, and from that point, I started to get downright worried. I mean, would they even know who I was anymore?

Most Important: Communication

The mentor's job is critical to the overseas employee and requires time, dedication, and innovative solutions to a difficult task. The most important tools available to the mentor today include a wide variety of communications media. Some techniques, such as electronic mail, are straightforward and easily implemented. The "magic of cyberspace" can help to bridge the gap between the expatriate and goings-on in the domestic office. It should be the responsibility of both the expat and the mentor to ensure that when technologically possible, the expatriate receives regular e-mail updates about corporate activities and "group gossip," in addition to normal interoffice mail. If electronic mail is not available, traditional interoffice mail should be enhanced to provide a modicum of connectedness. In addition, the employee should be given Internet access if it is available in the host country. All of these help overseas employees avoid the "exile syndrome" that many feel as the reality of physical separation from the domestic organization begins to sink in. (See "Interorganizational Transfers," page 164.)

> Company mail is fine, but what really helped keep me connected with my colleagues was e-mail. I took part in online discussions, read tech reports, and frankly did a lot of the same things I did when I was home. I can't imagine how I would have felt without it.

> Having Internet access allowed me access to massive amounts of information that just weren't available in-country [by traditional means]. The alternative would have been to get someone to send me the information by mail, and that just wouldn't have worked.

> Our company set up an internal Web site that only employees can access. It has HR information,

internal press releases, and all sorts of information. And because it's online, it can be accessed any time, regardless of time zone.

Formal Mentor Programs

Some multinationals have successfully implemented mentor programs for their overseas employees; among them are AT&T and 3M Corporation. (See the case study opposite.) When administered properly, as they are in these two corporations, mentor programs work well. To be truly effective, mentor programs must provide "soup-to-nuts" coverage—they must address both outbound and inbound considerations. Many corporations, for example, create programs that address only the outbound side of the move. Employees and their families are assigned a mentor who is responsible for putting them in touch with other families who have already been abroad, providing them with host country materials, and arranging language training and other related functions. Little, however, is done on the equally critical inbound side.

Another concern that is often expressed about mentor programs is the scope of the mentor's responsibility. Cathleen Dargy, an international human resources manager in San Francisco, has been involved in employee repatriation for some time. She observes that in many cases employees who are selected to be mentors for lower-level employees already have broad scopes of responsibility and may not be able to make the necessary commitment to

(Continued on p. 77)

Case Study:
AT&T Global Human Resources

One of the most effective expatriate employee management programs is administered by AT&T. In 1986, the company had 100 employees working abroad; today, it employs more than 800 expatriate Americans and 130 foreign nationals.

Before they go overseas, AT&T provides a one-day seminar for domestic employees that covers payroll, benefits, issues associated with expatriate living, and the like. It also provides information for families at this time.

AT&T employs a sponsorship program in which each expatriate employee is assigned a sponsor (mentor) who is typically two levels above them in AT&T's managerial hierarchy. The sponsor serves as a liaison between human resources and line management on behalf of the employee and ensures that the employee is kept in the corporate information loop, kept aware of changes at headquarters, and prepared properly for reentry at the appropriate time. The sponsor is required to stay in touch with the employee on at least a quarterly basis. Thanks to electronic mail, most employees stay in contact with their mentors considerably more frequently than that.

AT&T's compensation program is unique as well. Instead of paying a monthly incentive "add-on" to the paycheck while an employee is overseas, AT&T calculates an estimated incentive amount to be paid for the entire assignment and divides it into two pieces. Thirty percent is paid prior to the assignment as a mobility incentive. To receive it, the employee must submit a personal developmental growth plan that consists of three to five personal and professional goals to be achieved while abroad. This document is kept by and followed up on by HR personnel.

The remaining 70 percent is withheld for six months following the employee's return. During that time the employee must complete a report that tells AT&T what things should be done differently, how the transition could be better managed, and other job-related insights. The employee must successfully complete all aspects of the assignment to receive the completion bonus.

During the time that the employee is abroad, AT&T's Global Human Resources Department and the sponsor work with the employee to create a résumé that can be used to effectively "sell" the returning employee to a business unit.

When the time arrives for repatriation, AT&T provides a three-day seminar conducted by an independent consulting firm that specializes in cross-cultural transfers. The seminar includes individual programs for the employee, the spouse, and the children, followed by a final segment that is targeted at the family as a unit.

AT&T has also created an "alumni association" of international assignees that provides a support structure for those who have returned and an open forum for discussion of issues with prospective international employees.

the overseas employee. These people may have managerial responsibility for several hundred people worldwide, which dilutes their ability to be an effective mentor.

Corporate mentors, if employed, must recognize the importance of their role to their expatriate charges and treat the responsibility appropriately. If they do not feel that they will have the time or the ability to make this commitment, they should reconsider their decision to take it on:

> This [mentor job] is not a trivial task. It requires an *enormous* amount of work, much more than I anticipated. It's also not something that can be given a low-priority status. I realized pretty quickly that those folks really depend on you, and you'd better be there for them. It's not a job to be taken lightly, but boy, does it pay off.

> I had a mentor who frankly made my job in Brussels manageable. Without her, I never would have been as effective as I was. She made it a point to really understand my job, and the cultural challenges I had to deal with. She even bought a book about doing business in Belgium, and read it, cover to cover. When I came home, she arranged a staff meeting and invited me and the members of the group I was joining. Prior to my arrival, she briefed them on what I had been doing for the last two years, and then asked me to do a presentation on the role of the Brussels organization. It was great—I felt like she was really taking care of me.

Of course, the opposite is also true:

> The company appointed a mentor for me, but he turned out to be a bad choice for the job. He was a high-power executive type who was trying hard to move up in the organization, and I got relegated to a pretty low position in his priority food chain. I was pretty much on my own, and that caused problems for me that I don't even want to get into. My advice to potential mentors is this: If you don't think you have time to really do what the job demands, don't take it on. It's far too important to be ignored, because the people you support are too important to be ignored, as well.

Letters of Understanding

The negotiation process between an employee destined for an overseas position and the domestic organization that is placing the employee overseas is complex, and involves social, economic, and professional issues. Decisions and agreements need to be clearly defined in order to reduce stress and maximize the employee's chances of success in the international placement.

Many companies have found that a clearly articulated letter of understanding between the corporation and the employee can help ease the stress of the foreign assignment. Ideally, the letter should clearly define the expectations of both the company and the employee, and should make it very clear as to what the employee can expect upon their return with regard to position, responsibility, and compensation. The written plan that AT&T requires from employees is an example of this process. It asks employees to write a list of personal and professional goals that they will accomplish while overseas, and clearly defines the role of the mentor while the employee is abroad. Furthermore, it establishes the process by which the employee's résumé will be updated and circulated throughout the domestic corporation upon their return, and defines what steps the company will take to place the employee within the organization.

Obviously, this letter must be somewhat general in many areas, but some points can be clearly defined. Its primary purpose is to keep both the company and the employee on honest ground relative to each other. By clearly defining the roles of both parties, they are more apt to live up to the agreement. Because of this agreement, each must understand the other's situation, which improves the overall relationship. The employee and the employer should draft the letter jointly, but the employee's mentor often plays a key role in the creation of this document.

Points that should be addressed in a letter of understanding include the following:

- Employee compensation (base salary; incentive add-ons; bonuses; schedule of additional payments)

- Transportation of the employee and family to and from the host country assignment (time to wait for first home leave; frequency of home leaves)

- Schools for children, if applicable (tuition reimbursement for private schools, if necessary)
- Disposition of domestic residence (sell? lease?)
- In-country support (mentor; language lessons; acculturation seminars)
- Placement following repatriation (guaranteed position? specialized assignment?)

The format and content of a letter of understanding must be carefully thought out by both the employee and the corporation. Part of the initial discussion between the employee and their spouse should concern the factors that the letter should address:

> We talked to a lot of expatriates before we accepted the job, so we were lucky to have "the voice of experience" perched on our shoulders. We also spent a lot of time thinking and talking about the things we wanted the company to do for us to ensure that we didn't suffer financially as a consequence of taking…this job. So when the time came for negotiation, we were prepared. I can't emphasize enough how important it is to really wrestle with these things and talk about them early on.

Domestic Housing

A concern that often causes anxiety is what to do with one's home before going overseas. Employees often sell their homes prior to an overseas assignment.

(Continued on p. 83)

Resource:
Employee Relocation Council

The Employee Relocation Council (ERC) provides a wide variety of services to its members, including relocation research, a collection of relocation policies from hundreds of companies, job descriptions, relocation-oriented tax and legal information, a Relocation Career Hotline, a collection of publications that include *Mobility* Magazine, a network of relocation specialists, and a variety of professional relocation services offered by certified professionals in the field.

The organization provides three levels of service. Category One is directed at corporate relocation personnel and includes specific services such as home sale support and related issues, including mortgage assistance, tax legislation activity, and analysis of the effect of the transfer on employees and their families.

Category Two is targeted at relocation service companies. Its specific services include access to trends and practices studies in corporate relocation to help support the 500,000 employee transfers that occur annually and require nearly $15 billion in corporate relocation support.

Category Three provides services that are specific to real estate appraisers and brokers, and supports the unique requirements of appraisal fees, brokerage commissions, and service revenues that result from company-generated moves.

See the Appendix for more information about the Employee Relocation Council.

Resource:
Prudential Relocation Global Services

Prudential Relocation provides a complete suite of global relocation services. Since 1993 they have enjoyed a strategic alliance with Settler International, a subsidiary of Europ Assistance and the Generali Insurance Group. This allows Prudential to deliver relocation services to clients in more than seventy cities worldwide and to provide intercultural training services in more than 100 countries.

Prudential divides its services into six categories:

Business and Relocation Consulting:
- Intercultural business consulting and training
- Global relocation policy development

Pre-Departure Planning:
- Expatriation assessment and selection
- Assignment preparation
- Cultural orientation
- Intercultural seminars
- Language training
- Youth programs
- Visa and immigration service

Relocation Assistance:
- Home sale services
- Transportation of household goods
- Home management

Destination Services:
- School enrollment

> Local tours
> Assistance in finding a residence
> Utility connections
> Health care
> Bank accounts
> Insurance
> Driver's licenses
> Ongoing Assignment Support:
> > Family support services
> > Lease administration for local housing
> > Ongoing intercultural consulting
> Repatriation/Reassignment Services:
> > Repatriation and reassignment planning and consulting
> > Repatriation planning guides
> > Repatriation training programs
> > Repatriation reports on each family
>
> See the Appendix for additional information about Prudential Relocation Global Services.

In some cases this can be a serious mistake, as there are few investment instruments available that offer the same earnings potential as real estate.

If a family sells their house prior to expatriation and returns to live in the same or even a different city several years later, they may find that escalating home costs have priced them completely out of the market they were once in. Many expatriates come home and find that they either cannot afford to purchase a home at all, or must live in an area that is inconveniently distant from work.

When we were transferred to Milan from San Francisco, we sold our house in the East Bay, because we didn't know how long we'd be over there. Four years later, when we came home, we started looking at houses and realized that real estate had gone up in value so much that we could no longer afford to buy a house in the town where we lived before. Even though we invested the money we made on the house, it didn't come close to growing as fast as house values, so when we came back we ended up having to buy in a town that was twenty minutes farther out from the city. That was a very expensive lesson. My advice to other folks who followed us overseas was to keep their house and rent it—it's a bit of a pain, but well worth the aggravation.

Some companies go so far as to extend low-interest or interest-free loans to employees affected by this situation; they are far from the norm, however. Other corporations encourage employees to keep their homes and rent them while they are abroad, using employer-provided property management services. This protects the employee's investment and provides them with a readily available home when they return:

> One thing that is really important is to find a good property management company if you decide to rent your house while you're out of the country. I was worried that we'd come back to find our place "trashed" by tenants that didn't care as

> ### Resource:
> **Intercultural Press**
>
> Intercultural Press publishes books, videotapes, and educational support materials that focus on intercultural issues. These include generic cross-cultural awareness materials, support materials for cross-cultural trainers, guides for students in foreign study programs, materials focused on the challenges that face spouses and children, role-playing exercises, and country-specific resources.
>
> Clients of Intercultural Press include government agencies, multinational corporations throughout the world, schools, colleges and universities, students, and individuals who plan to move abroad.
>
> See the Appendix for additional information about Intercultural Press.

much about it as we did. Luckily, they were responsible people, and while they didn't take care of it as well as I would have, they didn't trash it, either. The company was good about screening tenants and matching them to our expectations.

Employees: Remember the Family

Prior to departure, employees should be individually and strongly counseled about the impact that the transition will have on their family. This concern is often overlooked: Once in-country, employees

> ***Resource:***
> **Air Animal®**
>
> One issue that is often overlooked when moving abroad is transportation of the family pet. Foreign requirements and restrictions on imported animals can be complex. Now there is at least one firm that specializes in international transportation of family pets.
>
> Air Animal® was founded by Walter and Millie Woolf in 1977 to satisfy the unique requirements of mobile families with pets. The business was formed as an outgrowth of the Woolfs' longstanding veterinary business in Florida. It now provides domestic and international pet transportation and management services. These services include the arrangement of pickup and delivery, move management and flight arrangements, kennels, boarding, and interstate and international health certificates.
>
> See the Appendix for more information about Air Animal.®

find themselves involved in the excitement and demands of work and forget that they have an equally important responsibility to their family. Their attention at home can go a long way toward effecting a successful family transition in the new culture:

> It really sneaks up on you. When we first got there, we were all wrapped up in the excitement of living

in such a new and interesting place. My wife spent her time meeting the other wives in the community, our kids got into school, and I got involved in work. The problem was that I got too involved. Let me tell you: Offshore jobs will take all that you're willing to give them, and more. Well, before long I was going in at 6:00, coming home long after dinner was over, sometimes after the kids were asleep. My wife had to sit me down for a talk before I realized what was going on.

It's insidious—watch out for it.

PREDEPARTURE CHECKLIST

Prior to departure, the corporation must arrange to move the employee, their family, and their belongings. This is a massively complex undertaking that comprises many steps. Here is a partial checklist:

Ensure that the employee and their family have arranged for all necessary passports and host-country visas.

Arrange to open both domestic and in-country bank accounts. Ensure that the two banks allow reciprocal transfers of funds.

Appoint a mentor and conduct predeparture transition awareness seminars.

If the corporation employs letters of understanding with its expatriate employees, ensure that there is one on file for the employee prior to departure. The mentor, supervisor, or human resources representative should review it carefully prior to departure.

Make travel arrangements for the employee, their family, and any pets. If a pet is involved, are there restrictions on bringing it into the host country? Is there a kennel or other boarding arrangement available? What veterinary certificates are required? Will the animal have to be quarantined upon arrival?

Provide the employee with a copy of the Centers for Disease Control's *Health Information for International Travel.*

Provide a list of items that they should carry with them. These might include seasonal clothing, medications or special dietary items, and special toys for young children. Check with expatriates or human resources employees who are familiar with the host country. Direct the family to books, current or former expatriates, and other resources that will help them assemble a list of personal items that they should purchase and take with them. As this list may vary widely from country to country, it would be wise to put the employee in touch with another in-country employee.

Arrange to pack, ship, and store the employee's personal household effects. Instruct the employee to create a detailed inventory of personal effects, including photographs or a videotape of all valuables, and make two copies. Store one copy in a safe-deposit box. Should loss or breakage occur, there will be a visual record of all valuables. Insurance companies strongly recommend this procedure.

Instruct the employee to request and travel with copies of medical records for all family members, including copies of prescriptions.

Instruct the employee to take ten to twelve loose passport photographs with them for each family member, as they are often required for national ID cards, residence permits, etc.

Instruct the employee to take marriage and birth certificates with them.

Instruct the employee to take a medical kit with any special medications.

If the employee has children, instruct the employee to ask school(s) for copies of each child's educational transcripts and other necessary documents. They will be required for matriculation abroad.

Provide the employee and their family with country information regarding living basics: banking; schools; churches; shopping; utility rates; housing options; medical care; driver's licenses; transportation options, including car availability; language training; and so forth. Arrange for an in-country contact person to meet the family upon their arrival to help them with both their immediate transition and the short-term transitional confusion that follows arrival. This person can be another expatriate, a local national, or both. In some cases several people might provide guidance to the newly arrived family.

Instruct the employee to update wills and to execute a power of attorney, if appropriate.

Help the employee, spouse, and older children secure international driving permits from an organization like AAA.

Have the employee check the power requirements of any appliances they intend to take overseas, since many countries rely on 220-volt, 50-Hertz electricity.

If the employee intends to take valuables with them overseas, they should be registered with Customs to prevent duty being assessed upon their return to the passport country. This is particularly true for imported items such as cameras, stereo equipment, and certain types of jewelry. U.S. Customs publishes a number of "Know Before You Go" documents that are helpful in this regard.

This is only a partial list; each country and each family's circumstances will pose unique requirements. The company (HR and line management), the mentor, and the employee should work together to ensure that all questions are resolved prior to departure, and the process should be controlled by the employee.

Summary

When the selection process is complete and the employee and their family are ready to prepare for expatriation, they should move deliberately and carefully. As part of the job negotiation process, the employee must ensure that they understand the nature of all benefits that will accrue as a result of accepting the position, as well as any added responsibilities. Both the employee and spouse should make a point of talking to current and former expatriates to get a firsthand understanding of any issues that they must address prior to departure or will face once they arrive in-country.

As part of the preparation process, the family should take whatever steps are necessary to acquaint themselves with the culture in which they will soon be immersed. These steps can minimize the impact of transition shock and will help start the expatriate experience on a positive note.

Questions for Review

1. How can a company use the W-curve model to prepare an employee for cross-cultural transition?

2. What specific training should domestic HR personnel receive if they are to select employees for overseas assignments?

3. What criteria should be employed by the corporation to select and train employee mentors?

4. What critical success factors must be in place for letters of understanding to succeed as a management tool?

5. What issues might be covered in a letter of understanding that are not mentioned in this chapter?

6. Under what circumstances might it be advisable for an employee to sell their home at the time of expatriation?

7. How might you find information about resources (besides those listed in this chapter) that support the activities of multinational corporations?

Notes

1. From Clyde N. Austin, *Cross-Cultural Reentry: A Book of Readings*. Originally excerpted from J. William Pfeiffer and John E. Jones (eds.), *The 1980 Annual Handbook for Group Facilitators* (San Diego, CA: University Associates, 1980).

2. Key Branaman Eakin, *The Foreign Service Teenager–At Home in the U.S.: A Few Thoughts for Parents Returning with Teenagers* (Washington, DC: Overseas Briefing Center, Foreign Service Institute, U.S. Department of State, 1988).

4

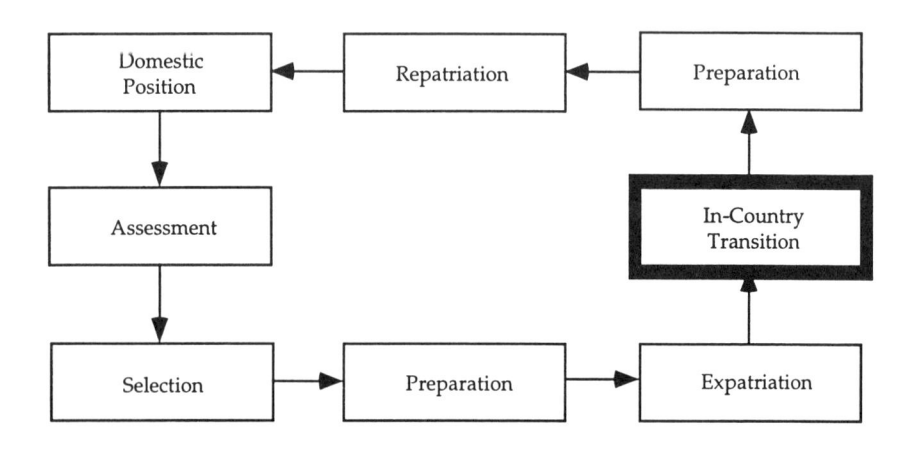

In-Country Transition

Domestic Position	←	Repatriation	←	Preparation
↓				↑
Assessment				**In-Country Transition**
↓				↑
Selection	→	Preparation	→	Expatriation

> *"Toto, I've a feeling we're not in Kansas anymore..."*
>
> *Dorothy,*
> *upon landing in Munchkindland*
>
> *From* The Wizard of Oz

Once the employee and their family have arrived in the host country, they must undergo the often wrenching adjustment to life in a different culture. At the family level, this period is characterized by gradual adaptation to the new culture, the stress of separation from familiar, comfortable surroundings and support structures, and an increased dependency upon other family members for emotional support. For the expatriate employee, there are the normal adjustment challenges of a new work location and peer group, plus adjustments that must be made with regard to language (particularly the local argot of business), cultural practices that affect business operations, and the intangible issues of the cross-cultural workplace.

In-country transition has three stages: initial orientation, a settling-in period, and ultimately, acceptance of life in the new country.

Arrival

The initial arrival in a new country is a dizzying, exciting, and complex experience. The sensual and cultural bombardment that occurs is a nonstop emotional vortex, and new expatriates often feel a strong sense of disorientation and "disconnectedness."

The company should ensure that expatriates have a provisional support structure during their first few weeks in the new country. The employee should be scheduled for some form of orientation at the office, and the family should be introduced to other families in the expatriate community. Spouses should be given the opportunity to ask questions, to visit schools if appropriate, to be coached in such seemingly commonplace skills as shopping, and to become acquainted with fundamental necessities such as medical care, churches, television and radio, social organizations, embassy or consular services, and other "second nature" items. If the spouse plans to seek employment in the host country, or if the company has arranged some form of employment, now is the time to begin the process.

Settling In

Adjustment to the new culture can be facilitated in two ways: by the expatriates and their approach to their new life, and by the company and its assistance. Some form of initial in-country orientation should be conducted to minimize the impact of transition:

> The month before I went to Cabinda [Angola], the company conducted a half-day orientation seminar that taught me the rules and regulations of life

in the [refinery] camp, what we were allowed to bring in, what medical requirements there were, and so on. Once I was there, they assigned me a "buddy" to show me around and acquaint me with the place. Human Resources provided a checklist so that I'd know what I was supposed to do once I got there. It was haphazard at best, but better than nothing.

General adjustment instructions should be part of the initial orientation. For example, expatriates should be counseled not to make the classic mistake of comparing the culture of the host country to that of the home country. As long as they approach their new country with an "it's not good or bad, it's just different" perspective, they will quickly learn to appreciate it for all that it has to offer. "Different" will not mean "bad"; it will simply mean...different.

Expatriates often fall into this trap: They compare their new culture to the one they left behind, and this can be destructive. When expatriates confront the initial cultural challenges of life in their host country, they often create a Xanadu-like image of home to help them deal with the difficulties of transition. This can become problematic when they return home, because the country that their nostalgic musings created doesn't exist:

> When we moved overseas, I was so glad to be leaving the heat, humidity, traffic, bugs, and cost of

living in Houston that it really didn't matter to me where we were going. After a couple of months in Saudi, though, I began to "pine" for home, and strangely enough I conveniently forgot all the things I used to hate there. All I could think of was barbecue, our house, the friends we left behind, and the beaches. It was like a little fantasy I created for myself, and while it was a nice image, it was way out of whack with reality.

I was so excited to be going home on our first home leave. We had been in Ghana for two years, and I was really looking forward to the food, the music, the cars, even the smells of the town that I remembered. But when we actually got there, it wasn't at all what I remembered. I was really disappointed—I felt let down. My parents, who had been stationed in several foreign posts before I was born, warned me about this [impact]. I didn't really pay attention; I wish I had, though.

This behavior is largely unavoidable and is a natural part of dealing with change. However, the employee and their family should be made aware of it so that they can minimize its impact as much as possible. Ongoing communication with the home office can help.

Acceptance

The final and most satisfying phase of the expatriate experience is acceptance of the local lifestyle.

This phase is usually marked by familiarity with and appreciation of the language and culture, recognition of all that the host country has to offer, development of friendships with local and expatriate residents alike, and acceptance of the expatriate lifestyle as normal and natural. It is also marked by a realization on the part of the expatriates that they have acquired a new set of skills that they didn't have before. These skills typically become an integral part of the person, and while they are tremendously enriching, they contribute to the difficulties encountered during reentry.

First Home Leave: Satisfaction and Conflict

The first sign of transition difficulties often appears during the first home leave. This is the first time the employee and their family return to their passport country, and the first time they face the culture they left behind. Once the initial euphoria fades, expatriates often realize that they are not the same people they were when they left home. They also begin to realize that their home is no longer in the passport country: It's back in the host country.

While there is always a certain amount of comfort in "going home," there are often just as many discomforts. Foods are different, and the abundance of so many items can make shopping an overwhelming experience. Friends and family seem to have changed; even driving is a new experience. The realization that "home" is no longer "home" can be disconcerting:

> I just couldn't believe it. I was looking forward to that trip so much—the chance to eat fast food, see some of my old friends, go to an English-speaking movie, drink root beer—that when I started to miss Wagga [Ouagadougou, Burkina Faso] it really set me back. I mean, here I was, back home again, doing the things I had been looking forward to for two years, and I was ready to leave after about a week. I just didn't get it.

Home visits, while usually reserved for vacations, can also be used by the employee as an opportunity to briefly "show their face" around the home office and to catch up on local goings-on. In many cases, however, expatriates use their vacation time to tour the regions of the world where they live, instead of going home. After all, they reason, this may be a once-in-a-lifetime opportunity that should not be missed.

One solution to this problem of "professional distance" is to *require* that employees and their families occasionally return home. Alternatively, employees can be brought home for meetings or short domestic assignments during their tenure abroad.

> It's pretty simple. In addition to home leave, we require our employees stationed offshore to come home *at least* once a year for meetings, briefing sessions, and status reports. It keeps us aware of what's going on in-country, and helps the employees stationed in foreign posts maintain their domestic office roots. It costs us a bit extra, but in

the seven years that we've been doing it, we've seen a marked improvement in the relationship between the domestic office and the offshore offices.

Two-Career Families

Two-career families create a special set of challenges for expatriates. In most countries it is difficult for a foreign national to secure permission to enter the local workforce. Clearly, if an employee is transferred abroad, their partner, if employed, must forgo their own career or remain behind—neither of which is acceptable.

Many families rely on the income generated by dual careers, and the loss of one paycheck due to an enforced international job transfer can be catastrophic.

Where feasible, some corporations have taken steps to provide employment for the spouses of employees they send overseas. Philip Morris uses the services of an outplacement firm to assist spouses of expatriate employees in their quests for possible job leads, while Eastman Kodak has a program designed to place spouses within the company or with other multinationals. The approach used by 3M is different, but effective: 3M provides spouses with a "dislocation allowance" to compensate them for their own losses when moving overseas. 3M recognizes that the allowance does not replace the salary that the spouse may have earned from a job at home, and that the family is adversely affected. The company also offers free tuition to spouses who wish to take college courses while abroad.

For spouses who do not work outside the home, the impact is somewhat less extreme. Even though they may not want a formal job, some spouses seek outside activities to keep them busy during the day. Within the expatriate community, for example, there are often paid or unpaid volunteer jobs available. Some spouses become involved in school activities as substitute teachers, library workers, or classroom aides. Churches often have a need for volunteers, as do service organizations such as men's or women's clubs. The company should collect a list of these activities and make it available to spouses.

The issues that expatriates face can have far-reaching and profound effects on lifestyle:

> We have friends who accepted a job in Thailand—that is to say, the husband's job was moved there from here [Dallas]. The wife worked, herself, and she had a pretty good job. They talked it over, though, and decided that the experience was worth the loss of her income. So she put her career on hold and they moved overseas.
>
> Now, they had postponed having kids, because they were a two-career couple. But once they'd been there for a while the wife began to feel isolated and bored, because she didn't work. So they decided to have children. Over the course of the five years that they've been in Bangkok, they've had two little girls.

In Thailand, every household has servants. In fact, the servants really raise those kids. Sheila can't even change a diaper without hurting somebody's feelings. So I have to wonder: What happens a year-and-a-half from now, when they come home and she has to take over? And what about the career she gave up—will she be able to go back? I've never been in that position, so I've never thought about the consequences. The problem is that I'm not sure she has either—and if not, I'm afraid she's in for a shock.

Summary

The three stages of in-country transition—initial orientation, settling in, and acceptance of the new lifestyle—take their toll on new expatriates. The first few weeks are often difficult and disorienting, but they can be made immensely easier by in-country liaison people who help the new arrivals get grounded.

Once the initial entry shock wears off, orientation and acceptance occur quickly. The local culture becomes familiar and the language easier to understand. Before long the expatriate no longer feels out of place. He or she feels at home.

Questions for Review

1. How should the corporation design a provisional support structure for the short-term, initial in-country transition period? How can the system be designed to properly support the needs of both the employee and their family?

2. How can the corporation help to lessen the impact of home leave?

3. "Repatriation starts when the employee first leaves their home country." Explain.

4. Which model is more effective for your corporation: an internal staff of counselors and expatriation specialists within the human resources department, or services contracted from outside firms? Explain.

5

Reentry

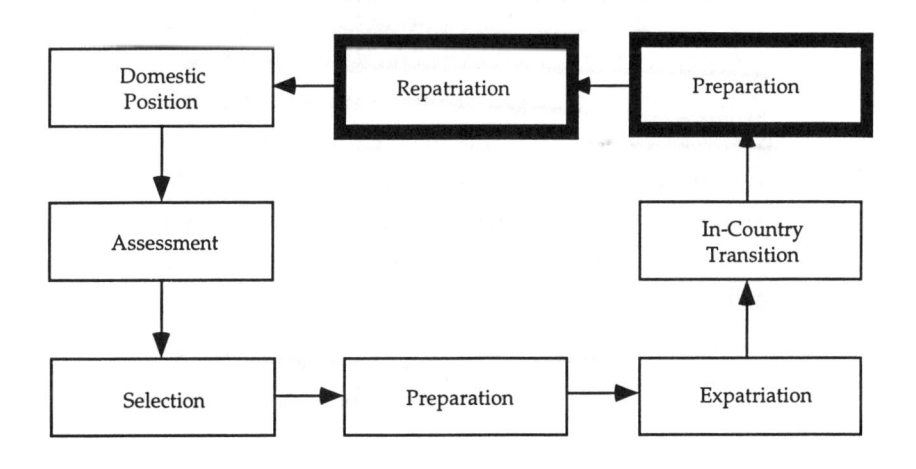

Domestic Position ← Repatriation ← Preparation

Domestic Position → Assessment → Selection → Preparation → Expatriation → In-Country Transition → Preparation

> *This is one of the lessons of travel—that some of the strangest races dwell next door to you at home.*
>
> Robert Louis Stevenson,
> Across the Plains
>
> *The very village was altered; it was larger and more populous. There were rows of houses which he had never seen before, and those which had been his familiar haunts had disappeared. Strange names were over the doors—strange faces at the windows—everything was strange. His mind now misgave him; he began to doubt whether both he and the world around him were not bewitched. Surely this was his native village, which he had left but the day before.*
>
> *From* Rip Van Winkle,
> *by Washington Irving*

By all accounts, the most difficult phase of the expatriate cycle begins with the journey home. When expatriates return to their passport country they often feel a deep and pervasive sense of loneliness and an overwhelming need to define themselves to their friends, families, and work acquaintances as much as to themselves. Attempts to relate to domestic peers often result in alienation as it becomes clear just how little the returning expatriate has in common with members of their new peer group. Attempts to describe experiences abroad can result in alienation as well, since people who have not experienced life abroad have no frame of reference and therefore no way to comprehend what the returnee describes. Repatriates are often branded as arrogant or as braggarts, constantly talking about their experiences abroad.

What domestic counterparts do not understand is that expatriates talk about the only life they know. They can't discuss local news, sports teams, favorite athletes, or teen rock music idols because during their time abroad they were not exposed to those influences. Expatriates who have returned usually learn fairly quickly that the disparity that exists between the two reality-based frames of reference is not bridgeable to a large extent, and they sometimes fall into the trap of retreating to the social sidelines because they feel out of place among their domestic peers:

> That was the most frustrating thing. I didn't feel any different from everyone else in the school when I enrolled, but that lasted about half a day. Some of the other students "adopted" me into their group, but I had a hard time relating to them because a lot of the time I didn't know what they were talking about. I really tried to fit in, but I just couldn't. It was like there was this big gap between us—I could really feel it.

This is when the mentor's role is most critical to the returning expatriate and their family. The mentor must now ensure that the employee's transition back to the domestic organization is smooth and productive, that the family's needs are looked after, and that the corporation's own requirements are met.

It cannot be stressed strongly enough that the return to the passport country must not be viewed as a rescue, any more than it should be viewed as a return "home": For the expatriate and their family, "home" will have all the frustrations and anxieties of another foreign assignment, albeit one that happens to have some familiar characteristics. The transition is no easier because it is to the passport country; if anything, it is more difficult because there may be expectations that it *will* be easy. The corporation must be sensitive to this and must prepare returning expatriates for the realities of reentry (see *Five Phases of the Global Nomad,* page 139).

Preparation for Reentry

Eventually the overseas assignment ends and the expatriates must return home. During the time that they are abroad, the family should prepare for this eventuality because repatriation is perhaps the most challenging period in the entire expatriate cycle. After an extended stay abroad the family has accepted the new lifestyle; they have made friends and may even consider the host country to be their home. The return to the passport country can therefore be wrenching and unsettling. To ease transition difficulties, the company should gradually prepare the employee and their family for the domestic lifestyle they will encounter when they return, and should begin this process as far in advance of the host country departure date as possible.

Several factors must be considered during this preparation process. It is a well-known fact that expatriates who accept the foreign lifestyle and embrace it (sometimes called "going native") often have the most difficult repatriation experiences.

Some companies recommend that expatriates undergo periodic counseling during home leave as part of the preparation for reentry. Others require that employees spend a certain amount of time during home leave at the office to ensure that they retain "hooks" with corporate lifestyle, maintain professional relationships, and stay aware of goings-on at headquarters. This practice gives management an opportunity to meet with the employee and to discuss any concerns they may have regarding placement, family issues, and the like. The mentor should guide this process.

Employees and their families must be counseled that some aspects of domestic life will be different when they return. Most expatriates won't be aware of this on their own, and if they are, they may deny the degree of potential impact. After all, they are returning to a perceived refuge: Their destination is *home*. This perception is a potentially dangerous one and should be tempered with a dose of careful reality. Both the employee and the family must be informed in advance of the differences that they will encounter, just as they were counseled when they originally went overseas.

The Repatriation Process

The most successful corporate repatriation programs are based on the assumption that a strong functional (and natural) linkage exists between the corporation's expatriation and repatriation strategies. The ideal program starts the repatriation process at the moment expatriation begins, by putting into place a support structure that starts to work when the foreign assignment begins. Its functional components include mentor/expatriate relationships, information feeds, feedback loops, mandatory meetings in the home office on a regularly scheduled basis, a plan for placement upon repatriation in a job that will use the expatriate's newfound international skills, and much more.

In too many cases, domestic human resources organizations treat repatriation as a form of rescue, one in which they are pulling the employee out of a hostile environment and bringing them home. In fact, the opposite is true: The host country is now *home;* the passport country is just another foreign assignment, with one significant exception. When the employee and their family left for their foreign post, the company helped them prepare for the transition by providing acculturation training, briefings about the host country, language lessons, personal contact with other expatriates, and general daily living information. These tools don't eliminate the shock of cross-cultural transition, but they minimize it and help make the experience as positive as possible for all concerned.

(Continued on p. 113)

Resource:
Consultants for International Living

Consultants for International Living (CIL) provides support services to expatriating and repatriating families. CIL believes that families prepared in advance for the rigors of cross-cultural transition will manage change better in their new environment.

CIL, whose clients are almost exclusively multinational corporations acting on behalf of their employees, uses a variety of techniques to prepare employees and their families for cultural transition. Prior to selection for a foreign assignment, CIL conducts suitability assessments for candidates and their families. These assessments measure psychological maturity and employee appropriateness based on family situation. CIL also provides consultation to the employee prior to selection and eventual departure. It works closely with the client company to align corporate goals with the employee assessment and selection process.

The organization also offers two-day reentry workshops for employees of client corporations in Europe, the Americas, and Asia. These Journey Home Workshops are typically conducted in the host country within a year prior to reentry. They address concerns such as psychological closure, personal readiness for reentry, and the physical logistics of repatriation.

Once the employee and their family have repatriated, CIL provides a Welcome Home Workshop that builds on the Journey Home Workshop. It is a dual-track program: employees receive professional employment counseling designed to help them take responsibility for finding a job. Family members receive individual guidance on domestic cultural reentry, school-related concerns, and employment counseling for the spouse who has been out of the workforce while abroad. The final phase of the Welcome Home Workshop is a common forum in which all members of the family may discuss their individual concerns.

Consultants for International Living also provides cultural awareness training for foreign nationals working in the United States for the first time and specialized training for domestic employees who manage overseas employees and their unique needs.

Dr. Frank Alagna, a principal in CIL and a former expatriate himself, says that the company's programs are carefully designed to be a positive educational experience. CIL does not want participants to feel as if they are undergoing therapy or being treated for some kind of mental health problem. As a consequence of this approach, employees and their families usually embrace the process enthusiastically and derive considerable benefit from the training.

"There is an interesting trend under way in corporations today," says Alagna.

> For the first time, multinational corporations recognize how profoundly important it is for the

> employee's family to be happy, especially in an offshore post. If the family is content and comfortable, the employee will be as well, and will be able to devote the appropriate amount of time to the job. If the family is unhappy, however, the employee's loyalties will be split between family and work, and their productivity will be severely affected.
>
> See the Appendix for more information about Consultants for International Living.

Failure to provide a similar level of support on the reentry side of the equation is a recipe for failure and can lead to large losses for the corporation. Studies indicate that a high percentage of returned expatriates quit their jobs within the first two years following repatriation, and the reason most often cited for their departure is failure of the company to repatriate and assimilate them properly.

The knowledgeable international human resources organization takes appropriate steps to reduce the impact of reentry. These organizations often rely on mentors and staff counselors to guide the repatriation of returning employees. They employ checklists, timelines, and responsibility matrices, and work carefully with line management to ease the stress of reentry for the employee and their family.

Some corporations hire specialists in international workforce management to help them administer their overseas personnel operations. They in turn employ relocation specialists, property managers, industrial psychologists, counselors, educators, specialists in international law, and other professionals to help expatriates with the myriad details that confront them during their cross-cultural transition. They work closely with employees and help them manage the issues they will face on both the outbound and inbound sides of their journey.

CHECKLIST: PREPARATION FOR REENTRY

When the foreign assignment comes to a close and repatriation is imminent, the employee and their family should prepare for reentry. The following list of preparatory activities is based on interviews with former expatriates and their employers.

Before Returning Home

As a family, discuss the worries, concerns, fears, and issues that all family members have. Be aware of and sensitive to each other's concerns.

As an employee, consider the same worries, concerns, fears, and issues, but from a professional point of view. Discuss them with your mentor if you have one; if not, discuss them with supervisors, former expatriates, and human resources personnel. Make sure that you have access to current trade journals, corporate newsletters, placement information, World Wide Web sites, and other material that will help you prepare for the transition to the home office.

Call, write, or send e-mail to friends and colleagues who hold domestic positions, and ask them about "life at headquarters." Get "tuned in" to things at home. If you have access to e-mail, use it to subscribe to and take part in chat groups or online services that will facilitate your acclimatization. If your company has a public

Web presence or a corporate intranet, explore its content and familiarize yourself with the information it contains.

Keep a journal while overseas. Write down feelings, concerns, regrets, emotions, and happy moments. Record questions that need answers. Keep track of how you used your time while overseas. This information can be invaluable later on, when the difficulties of reentry begin to surface.

Subscribe to and read magazines, newspapers, and other literature from the city to which you will be returning, or have someone in that city—perhaps the mentor—send you current copies on a regular basis. Study the living and lifestyle sections, and familiarize yourself with real estate listings and costs. Scan the community's Web page, if they have one. Call or write to the Better Business Bureau in the community for an information package.

On the basis of personal research and information provided by your company, prepare a tentative family budget.

If you are a parent, be sensitive to the fact that the change in lifestyle can be traumatic for children, particularly for teens. The transition from a domestic public school to an overseas private school and back again can be difficult. Overseas schools are often more structured, tend to have smaller student/teacher ratios, and usually become more of a tight-knit community than stateside schools. When students enroll in school, take time to meet with teachers to help them understand the emotional stresses that your children will experience. Among their peers, they may initially be viewed as odd or different owing to unfamiliar clothing styles, accent and language nuances, or lack of familiarity with cultural icons. Arrange with teachers to have young children do a presentation about their experiences to the rest of the class, as these activities can help narrow the cultural gap that will inevitably exist. For more on this subject, see *Part 6: The Special Case of Expatriate Children.*

Be aware of the physical and emotional burdens you will encounter upon your return. Be especially sensitive to the needs of your family: Their transition will be at least as difficult as yours.

If you are married, prepare for the impact on your spouse.

If possible, allow for a transition period between the departure from the foreign post and the return home in order to mentally prepare for the transition. Take a vacation (a *real* vacation, just for the family, not a working one).

Take the time to say good-bye to friends. Many people fall into the trap of avoiding good-byes because they are so much a part of expatriate life and are so painful. This is a mistake and can lead to sadness and guilt later on. *Say good-bye.*

When they return home, many expatriates express regret over the fact that they did not take the time while overseas to become familiar with their host country. They recommend avoiding these regrets by making an effort to get to know the local people, their culture, their lives. Learn the language well. *Travel while in-country and make an effort to see as much of the country as possible. This is, after all, an opportunity that may not come again. It is an educational experience that shouldn't be missed; the entire family should take advantage of it.*

Breaking Ground: The Domestic Workplace

If the employee is sent overseas because of certain specific skills that will be valuable in the host country, they should be repatriated with the same philosophy in mind. The experience abroad provides them with skills that should be put to use by the corporation when they return. The company should make every possible effort to place the employee in a position that will make the best use of these capabilities. Overseas operations are expensive; why not get the most out of the investment? If the employee is not properly placed, statistics indicate that they will likely leave within two years. Why take that chance?

> It didn't matter what I did, who I talked to, or what I volunteered to get involved in. Nobody seemed to care that I was worth more to them when I came back from Europe than I was when I left. After about nine months of beating my head against the wall, I finally threw my hands up. I put my name and résumé on the street, and within three days I had multinationals all over me. I was gone a month later.
>
> The funny thing is that when they called me in for my exit interview, and I told them bluntly why I was leaving, they didn't get it. They didn't have a clue.

Similarly, if an employee is sent overseas in a developmental assignment to prepare them for a higher position within the company, then the company should follow through with its commitment and have a documented, well-understood plan on file for that employee, to be implemented upon their return.

Companies typically employ one of two strategies to reintegrate their returning expatriates into the domestic workplace. The first is an informal process, in which employees are simply brought home and placed in a "waiting for work" queue until the right job is found or created for them. Alternatively, the company may keep the employee overseas until a position is found.

In some cases the employee will simply be placed in any available job or may even be let go. Some overseas positions are temporary; when the assignment ends, so does employment with that corporation. One recent survey showed that 65 percent of returned expatriates are not guaranteed a job by their company.

The alternative process is a more formal one in which the employee's mentor carries out the company's expatriate sponsorship program and safeguards the employee's welfare, both while they are abroad and when they return. In this approach, the expatriate is tracked carefully while overseas, using a system that not only manages technical knowledge and human resources issues but also tracks enhanced skills acquired while overseas. This information is later used to match the employee to a job that can best use their unique knowledge and capabilities.

AT&T's repatriation technique is an example of this process.

Under the guidelines of a formal repatriation scheme the employee knows what job or type of job they will return to. Prior to their return, their résumé is circulated throughout the organization to advertise their imminent availability in the event that their specific skills are in demand:

> I was concerned about what I would be doing when I got back, because I really got to like the international aspects of my job. Well, Jim [the mentor] really took care of me. Three months before my planned arrival, he called up all kinds of people in various international groups in the company, sent them my résumé, and told them that I'd be available in November. When I arrived, I already had interviews lined up, and the best part is that four of the five were along the lines of what I was looking for. In fact, I accepted the second offer.
>
> I can't tell you how valuable that was. It saved me a lot of wheel-spinning that I would have had to do if he hadn't already greased the skids for me.

Because the move overseas often involves a transfer between the domestic and international organizations of the parent company, it is important that there be a positive and understanding relationship between the two. If the employee returns home and there is no position waiting for them, the domestic and international organizations should collaborate to find a challenging job for the returning employee.

Professional Transition

Ideally, the company should have an assignment or project for the returnee to take on in order to facilitate the professional transition between organizations. The project should be challenging and should make use of the skills the employee acquired while abroad. In some companies the returnee's first task is to write a "trip report" that serves several purposes. First, it serves as a debriefing or turnover document for the organization in general and for the employee's successor in the overseas position, if there is one. Second, it gives the employee an opportunity to document newfound skills and capabilities, which are then reflected in their professional résumé. Finally, it gives the employee the opportunity to address issues about the company's management of overseas employees. For example, the employee may have recommendations for the human resources department that will improve its methods for managing expatriate employees.

At AT&T, this document must be completed and delivered formally; its completion is a condition for payment of the remaining at-risk money that was part of the initial agreement between AT&T and the employee. AT&T's Global Human Resources Department takes this process seriously: It encourages employees to be candid and frank in their reports, particularly if their comments address tangible issues. As one employee observed,

> I knew I had to write this [trip report] when I got back, but I figured it was just a formality and that it would end up in a drawer somewhere, filed away forever. Well, they surprised me: Two weeks after I gave my report—which was long and detailed, by the way—to my mentor, my phone rang. It was a manager in HR who wanted to talk about my comments. Well, that was just the beginning. I came home nearly two years ago, and I still get calls from those people. And I'm not unique: I've become part of the "domestic expats club" in the company, and they *all* get calls periodically. It's a nice feeling to know that what we think matters, and that they value what we have to say.

If possible, a similar program should be created for the employee's family members. If another family is about to depart, for example, the company, through the mentor, should arrange for spouses and children to meet and discuss the transition. This can have a dual impact. First, it acquaints the outgoing family with expatriate life from a recent, firsthand point of view. Second, it helps accelerate reentry for the returning family.

The process of reentry is not easy. Families often feel pressure from their domestic peers to "change more quickly" and to "get back to being who they were before they left." They can't, of course, because they're not the same people they were when they left, any more than their peers are. Unfortunately, many expatriates try to accelerate the process artificially. Teenagers sometimes try to "go native" by immersing themselves in the local scene, a process that sometimes (but not always) leads to problems. Similarly, peer pressure to "change back to normal" can exacerbate feelings of disconnectedness:

> I've lived in the States since 1983, and even though I live in America and have taken on U.S. citizenship, deep down I'm still English. When I visit friends and family in England, though, they are quick to observe that I'm "different." And when I go home to the States, my friends there say the same thing because I speak with an accent, I use unfamiliar words for things, and so on. I'm like a man without a country—I'm not English, and I'm not American. So what am I? *That's* when the sense of isolation and being disconnected kicks in, and it can led to a real feeling of loneliness. Believe me: The multicultural lifestyle is a wonderful experience, but it's a bit of a mixed blessing.

Returned expatriates must understand that their international experience is important and should not be expunged. Many former expatriates have expressed deep regrets years after their return from abroad because they worked hard to shed their "foreignness" to fit into the domestic scene more quickly.

Summary

It isn't possible to completely eliminate the challenges of cross-cultural transition. However, both the company and the employee can take steps to minimize them. Most important is to recognize what they are, what causes them, how to manage their impact, and how to turn them into positive forces rather than negative ones. There are specific things that the company and the employee can do; some of them are described below.

Company Responsibilities. The responsible company should design and put into place a formal repatriation program. It should be designed either by human resources personnel who have lived overseas themselves, or by HR employees under the direction of former expatriates. The program should comprise more than a "welcome home" ceremony; it should be serious in its approach and carefully crafted to cover all important issues, and long enough to have a tangible impact. It should be attended by the returning employee, the family, and the mentor.

Employee Responsibilities. Be who you are. Don't try to become a "regular person" overnight. You aren't a regular person; you are a unique individual. Don't discard the richness and values that became part of you during your stay overseas. It takes time to learn the music, the "cultural top forty," and the speech and dress patterns of a new place. Give yourself time. *There's nothing wrong with you.*

Try to get in touch with people who know who you are and who understand you. Spend time with other expatriates who have been home for a while; ask them for tips on how to deal with the feelings of exclusion and indifference that are often part of coming home. Enroll your kids in youth programs that will help them become socially integrated and make friends.

CHECKLIST: REENTRY

Prior to reentry, the company and the employee should work together to ensure that the following preparatory steps are taken as necessary. This process should be coordinated between the employee, the human resources department, and the mentor.

Company Responsibilities

Arrange for temporary housing for the employee and his or her family, if necessary. If the family is returning to the same city they left, and if they retained ownership of a home, arrange through the property management company for the home to be vacant and ready to be occupied when they return. If they are returning to a different city, provide a list of local realtors, as well as a list of realtors in the original city, if the employee plans to buy a home in the new location. If the company has a home sale program, put the employee in touch with it.

Work with the employee to ensure that change-of-address notifications are sent properly. Provide a list of "commonly overlooked" addresses.

Provide the employee with a complete list of community publications, newspapers, magazines, and useful local contacts.

Discuss such issues as utility rates and general costs of living with the employee and their spouse. Keep in mind that if the employee has been out of the passport country for any length of time, these costs may have changed dramatically.

Inform the employee of the proper procedures for securing a driver's license, registering a vehicle, etc.

Notify the employee about medical care issues: nearest hospital, pharmacies, special services that might have come about since they left, etc.

Provide career counseling or a list of providers to the returning spouse. If the spouse plans to work, inform them of available child-care options.

Provide the family with a list of local school options: public, private, religious or parochial, etc. If returning teens are about to attend college, arrange for academic counseling to help them with the transition.

Conduct an orientation session about shopping, grocery stores, discount/membership department stores, banks, malls, utilities, etc.

If the employee retained ownership of a home while abroad, give them a list of service providers: cleaners, painters, maintenance services, landscapers, pest control, etc.

Employee Responsibilities

Arrange for copies of medical records from foreign medical service providers to be sent home.

Arrange for any inoculations that might be required for reentry.

Arrange for children's school records to be sent to their new school.

If a pet is involved, arrange for transportation, as well as any necessary shots, quarantine, or paperwork.

Send change-of-address notices; check with company-provided list to ensure that none are forgotten.

List, photograph, or videotape all valuables prior to shipment.

Close all local bank accounts, and arrange to open new ones at home.

Once home, remember the following: savings account; checking account; safe-deposit box; ATM cards; voter registration; library cards; driver's licenses; medical and dental plan forms; etc.

Get addresses and phone numbers of friends and acquaintances before departing the host country.

Say good-bye.

Questions for Review

1. Discuss ways in which the mentor can help ease reentry for the employee.

2. What role should the mentor play in the family's repatriation?

3. Should corporations create separate global human resources organizations that are functionally separate from domestic human resources departments? Why or why not?

4. Imagine that you are a domestic manager about to receive a newly returned expatriate employee into your work group. What do you want to know about the person? What might you discuss in your initial meeting with the individual? How will you prepare your other subordinates for the arrival of the new employee?

5. What steps can be taken to guarantee that the employee's "trip report" is used appropriately and acted upon effectively?

6. Comment on the following statement: "Reentry doesn't begin upon arrival in the home country or at the conclusion of an international assignment. It begins when the expatriate *leaves* the *home* country, and concludes successfully upon their *return* to the home country."

6

The Special Case of Expatriate Children

A gut sense that I do not have a rightful place in any setting, that I do not quite fit in, and that I have no right to shape what goes on, not being a proper member, is a...bestowal of my upbringing. I will ever have this shade of vulnerability. I will always live along in discomfort, certain that, in order to fit into a group or place in which I have set myself down, I must change something deep and vague and essential in myself. This perspective affords one the sense of...standing outside, always looking in.

It is the longing for America, of course, that takes up the largest space in the trunk of my traveling childhood. Like a bulky winter coat jammed on top, it cloaks the other items in the trunk. Yearning for ritual and community and belonging is the horse I ride.

I have lost something sweet and irreplaceable.

But another thing is equally true. I have sauntered away with riches.

> A...legacy of my upbringing is that I am, by inmost nature, a chameleon, a sponge, a being of multiple selves. When I arrive anywhere I observe the mores and values of the place and then seek to mimic them, becoming, in a sense, each time, someone new.
>
> *from* Longing for America:
> Notes from a Traveling Childhood,
> *by Sara Mansfield Taber*

Children are most profoundly affected by cross-cultural reentry, particularly those who spend their teen years abroad. Sociologists have studied the impact of cross-cultural transition on children for years, and the results of their studies are provocative. Dr. Ruth Useem of Michigan State University[1] studied 150 children who had lived overseas for parts of their lives and found that virtually none of them wanted a career that would keep them exclusively in the United States. Twenty-five percent knew the country where they wanted to live and work; 29 percent wanted a job that would keep them overseas but would move them from country to country; 25 percent wanted to be based in the United States with occasional trips abroad; and 12 percent wanted to work in the States but have regular opportunities to work outside the country.

For several decades Useem and her husband, both sociologists at Michigan State University, have researched third culture kids (TCKs)[2]—children who experienced an international/multicultural childhood, usually because of their parents' work—and discovered that the experience of living in a culture but not belonging to it can transform a person in profound and far-reaching ways. One writer[3] summed up the qualities of TCKs this way:

> They have superior (skills) of diplomacy, flexibility, linguistic ability, patience, and sophistication. On the downside, there's insecurity in relationships, unresolved grief stemming from constantly leaving friends throughout childhood, and rootlessness.

One young lady who had recently returned from several years abroad with her parents observed this about herself and her peers:

> We become flexible, and learn to adapt immediately to everyone else's behavior patterns. After awhile, though, you lose track of who you are, since you've spent so much time and energy being what other people want you to be and trying to fit into the local lifestyle. It becomes difficult to judge right from wrong, good from bad. Because we were taught not to be judgmental about the places we lived, and because we didn't really fit in completely anywhere, we became completely accepting. Things just are.

In 1976 S. L. Werkman and F. Johnson[4] compared the differences in values and attitudes between teenagers raised in the United States and those raised abroad. They found that children raised abroad generally tend to be less optimistic about the future and less secure in life than their domestic peers. Moreover, loneliness and restlessness don't appear to bother them as much, and they tend to place less importance on close friendships than their domestic counterparts do:

> I never allowed myself to establish close friendships while we were living overseas. I didn't know it back then, of course, but now I realize that it was probably some sort of protection mechanism. I guess I got tired of having to say good-bye to close friends, so I just withdrew a little bit and quit getting so close to people.

Psychologists agree that these results do not indicate that children raised abroad are less "psychologically robust" or healthy than children raised in the States, but that the experience of living abroad does have an impact.

Useem's study concludes that of the children studied, 7 percent claimed to feel at home with their domestic peers, while 74 percent felt most comfortable with other TCKs or people who had lived overseas.

The interviews conducted during the preparation of this book reveal that, by and large, TCKs value diversity and are strongly attracted to interracial and intercultural groups. They tend to seek out these groups and become socially involved with them, and often seek later employment that will allow them to serve as a bridge for foreign nationals in the workplace:

> I remember parties at embassies and private homes where attendees were often from different countries and language groups. I often stood and marveled at the facility with which my friends, many of them long-term expatriate children, moved from conversation group to conversation group, effortlessly and unconsciously shedding one cultural skin and language for another.

As the global workforce emerges, the Global Nomad model can be extended to adults who are employed abroad. Figure 6-2 illustrates the slightly different set of influences that affects the employee. Note

(Continued on p. 138)

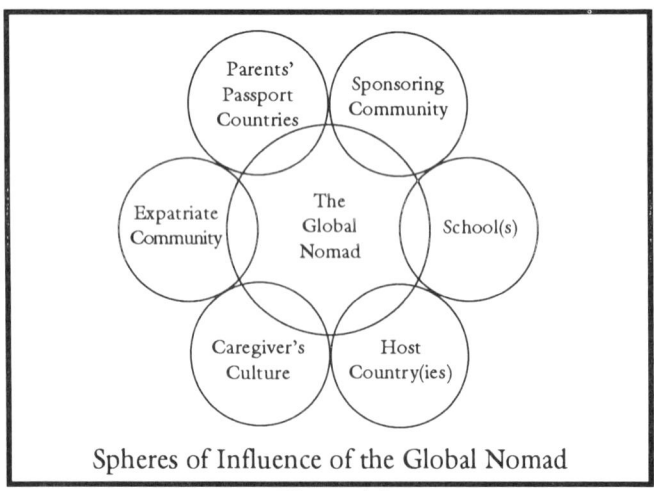

Spheres of Influence of the Global Nomad
- Parents' Passport Countries
- Sponsoring Community
- Expatriate Community
- The Global Nomad
- School(s)
- Caregiver's Culture
- Host Country(ies)

Figure 6-1
Courtesy Global Nomads International, Inc.

Resource:
Global Nomads International, Inc.

Norma McCaig, founder of Global Nomads International, Inc. (GNI), has observed that the long-term impact of international living on children of expatriate professionals can be intense. According to McCaig, a global nomad is "a person who had an internationally mobile childhood due to their parents' work."

McCaig founded Global Nomads in 1986

> as a not-for-profit organization dedicated to providing a forum for affirmation of the value of an internationally mobile childhood, by joining other global nomads to share experiences and ideas; to explore the lifelong impact of this experience through discussions, conferences, workshops, publications, and tapes; and for action to apply intercultural and linguistic skills, global awareness, and appreciation of diversity to benefit ourselves, the global nomad community, and broader local, national, and international communities. In 1993, GNI became affiliated with the United Nations as a non-governmental organization.[5]

McCaig is a global nomad herself. Because her father worked for a multinational pharmaceuticals company, she spent eleven years in the Philippines, a year-and-a-half in Sri Lanka, and two years in India, and completed her international

> tour with a one-year return to the Philippines for her senior year of high school.
>
> When she was in her mid-thirties, McCaig began to ponder the difficulties she had experienced after her return to the United States. She spoke with other former expatriates and, after considerable research, discovered that she wasn't alone in her feelings.
>
> When she founded Global Nomads International, she did so with an understanding that the global nomad is surrounded and affected by multiple "spheres of cultural influence," as illustrated in Figure 6-1. These include the parents' passport country(ies), the expatriate community, the culture of the host country, the local school culture, the influence of a domestic caregiver in the home, and the influence of a sponsoring community, as occurs in the case of missionary children or children who take part in a "junior year abroad" program. These cultural forces combine to create a rich and complex childhood experience that has a profound and long-lasting impact.

that the passport country, the expatriate community, and the host country are still important parts of the model; to them, add the mentor's influence, the cultures of both the domestic and overseas corporations, family responsibilities, and a set of intangible forces such as concerns about continued employment and managerial responsibilities following repatriation.

Spheres of Influence of the Corporate Global Nomad

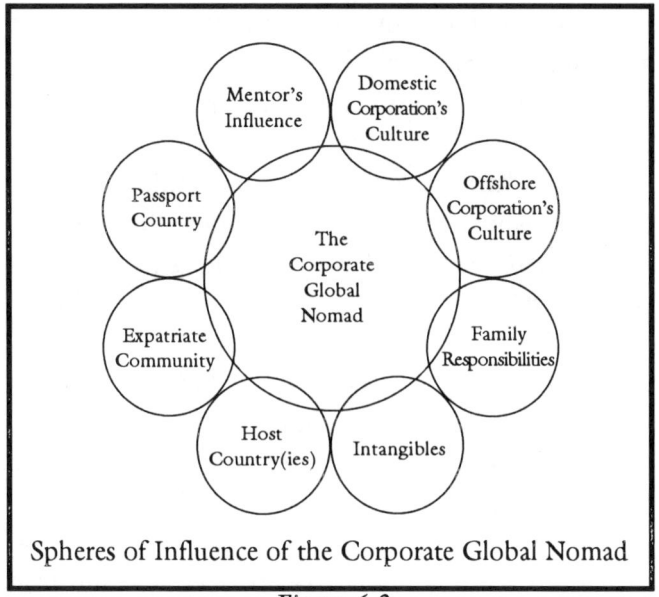

Figure 6-2

Five Phases of the Global Nomad

Norma McCaig identifies five phases that individuals, particularly children, go through during the transition into the role of a global nomad.

In the first stage, children become *cultural sponges.* Everything about their new lifestyle and culture is refreshing and exciting, and they soak it up, take it in, internalize it. This phase takes place in the host country and usually passes quickly.

In the second stage, children become *cultural chameleons,* also known as "participant observers." They continue to watch the world around them and continue to learn, but the initial shock has worn off and they begin to take part in the new lifestyle with minimal trepidation or self-consciousness. Soon they assimilate comfortably into their new world. Like the previous stage, this one takes place in the host country.

The third phase begins when children return to the passport country. In this stage they become *hidden immigrants*. This is a challenging time that is difficult to negotiate and can result in problems later if the child does not have help in understanding what is happening. The child has returned "home," only to discover that the passport country isn't really home: the country they *came* from is. To the child, the passport country is just another foreign place, causing some researchers to conclude that the term "reentry" is not really accurate and that "entry" is a far more appropriate word. Of course, to the folks back home the child and their family have been "rescued" and have finally returned to a place where they can feel safe and secure—clearly an erroneous but all too understandable conclusion. The child is, in reality, a hidden immigrant.

Children who are able to successfully negotiate the rocky shoals of the hidden immigrant stage pass on to become *transnationalists*. They begin to understand that their roots span multiple cultures and that they may be able to take advantage of the fact. They speak several languages, are comfortable in the presence of diverse cultures, and are tremendously adaptable to changes in their surroundings. They begin to feel a sense of control and to feel as if they can make a difference within their sphere of influence.

In the final stage, children become *world citizens*. During this stage they may choose to become an expatriate later in life and may begin to feel that it is acceptable and in fact desirable to have a global perspective rather than an ethnocentric one. They may become emotionally and politically attuned to a far broader set of cultures than those provided by their home environment. They may explore diverse religions, get involved in social issues, and pursue careers that will once again take them overseas.

An indication of the need for a shared forum for global nomads is the expansion of Global Nomads International. GNI branches have been founded in Washington, D.C., Boston, Atlanta, New York, and San Francisco, as well as in Norway and Switzerland. Groups have also been formed on college campuses, among them George Mason University, George Washington University, the University of Pittsburgh, Duke University, Valparaiso University, and the University of Michigan, Ann Arbor.[6]

Organizations like Global Nomads International can provide support for children who are going through the difficulties of reentry. Preparation for reentry, however, is crucially important. The impact of repatriation and reassimilation cannot be overstated.

Preparing Children for Reentry

Each age group presents its own set of challenges that parents must be sensitive to if they are to help children weather the difficult passage between cultures.

Through awareness, parents can anticipate the problems that each child will encounter; by being sensitive to them and responding appropriately, parents can help ease the pain of transition.

While the information that follows is primarily for parents, the corporation should ensure that employees who are embarking on an overseas assignment are aware of the issues associated with "transnational parenting."

Babies and Toddlers

Generally speaking, younger children are less affected by cross-cultural transition than older children. The world of younger children tends to revolve around their parents, while older children are usually part of well-developed social structures. Babies and toddlers, while not particularly easy to travel with, do not have an extensive social life outside the home and therefore tend to weather entry and reentry well:

> Naturally, we were concerned about our [two-year-old] daughter when we moved. As it turned out, it wasn't a problem. As near as we could tell, she was still young enough that all the change didn't bother her that much. As long as we were around—which was no different than at home [in Vancouver], she was fine. In fact, she adjusted faster than all of us, if her language skills were any indication.

Middle Childhood

For some children, particularly those who have not yet reached their teen years, personal possessions can be as important as friendships. Parents should prepare these children for the move abroad by instructing them to select certain possessions that they will take with them on the trip, and help them understand that while their remaining possessions will be packed, perhaps for a very long time, they will eventually be reunited with them:

> Just before we left, Mom gave each of us a carryon bag and told us to stuff it with our most important things. She didn't tell us why, and she didn't put any limits on what could go in the bag. She and Dad went through what we packed later and offered some suggestions about things that we might have forgotten. They didn't ask us to take anything out, though.
>
> In the end, that was a great idea. When we got to Barcelona, the four of us were crammed into a tiny apartment downtown for three months until we found a house. If we hadn't had those toys, our parents probably would have killed us.

While younger children do develop close friendships, they typically have not yet developed sophisticated social skills. As a result, they may have trouble meeting other children in the new country and may require "parental intervention" to help them overcome the awkwardness of first encounters. Parents must remember that the transition is as difficult for the child as it is for them; any help the parent can lend early in the process can go a long way toward helping the child assimilate more quickly into the new culture. Again, a frank discussion with the teacher to help them understand what the child is feeling can be helpful:

> Two weeks after we arrived, my new boss invited us over to his house for an afternoon pool party. It turned out that he had three daughters who were exactly the same ages as our sons. All the kids were a little awkward at first, but by the end of the evening they were fine with each other. That really took an edge off for the boys when they enrolled in school a week later. They already had friends, and that made it easier for them to ease into some new social circles.

Teens

One of the best guides on reentry for parents of teenagers is *The Foreign Service Teenager—At Home in the U.S.: A Few Thoughts for Parents Returning with Teenagers,* by Kay Branaman Eakin.[7] While targeted specifically at the children of American Foreign Service employees, the booklet is filled with useful information that, to a large extent, is universally applicable. Eakin discusses major issues that confront teens today, suggests techniques for dealing with them, and provides worksheets that the family can use to prepare for their reentry.

Teens are particularly hard-hit by reentry. In addition to the trauma of dislocation and reorientation, they are usually undergoing major social and physical changes as well. Their bodies are developing, and they are becoming functionally independent as they go through the transition to young adulthood. The teen years are difficult enough without the added strain imposed by a cross-cultural shift in lifestyle.

Sometimes seemingly minor things can pose the most drastic problems to the teen following reentry. Most expatriate teens have never had a driver's license or a part-time job, since they are often unavailable in the host country. When they attempt to enter the domestic peer group, this disparity can lead to difficulties, as many of their peers may have been working and driving for some time.

> I was kind of embarrassed. During the summer, I came home for college and got my first driver's license, and then got a job—my first job, by the way—in a carwash. I had never learned how to drive overseas, because where we lived you couldn't drive until you were twenty-one. So there were only certain things I could do there, because I wasn't comfortable driving all those different cars

around. The other kids had been driving since they were sixteen, so it was second nature to them. I was an oddball.

Parents should anticipate these concerns and make arrangements for driving lessons and part-time work when the teen is ready.

One parent described an additional problem that her son experienced. Because the boy had spent a great deal of his childhood in transition, he reached a point where he refused to "settle in." He began to treat everyday life as if each day might be his last in a particular place. He therefore never made long-range or even medium-range plans, since events beyond his control could change them at any time. This tendency to avoid commitments caused problems for the boy when he went off to college, and later when he joined the workforce. He became indecisive, preferring to let others make decisions. According to the boy's mother, it took him quite a few years to overcome this behavior.

Supervision

Children of overseas employees tend to have less supervision in their daily lives than their domestic peers. They are often free to roam the city with their friends, use public transportation, even go away for unsupervised weekend trips. There are various reasons for this. In some cases, the local culture guarantees a level of safety for children that is not available at home; in others, parents and children simply live different lives because of work or social obligations. Whatever the reason, children who return to the often more rigidly structured domestic culture can feel stifled, unreasonably restricted, even punished, in much the same way that their parents do when they return to an overly bureaucratic domestic position after working abroad:

> It took me a long time to get used to the fact that I couldn't just go anywhere I wanted to in New York, the way I was used to doing in Spain. Over there, we could go anywhere we wanted, just about anytime we wanted, and no one would bother us. Here, I had to learn a whole new set of rules and, frankly, it irritated me. I missed the freedom I had in Spain.

Because expatriate children live in a world of constant change, they are often denied many of the points of stability that they need in their lives. Parents must work to provide stability consistently and fairly, and realize that the members of an expatriate family usually draw closer while overseas and must learn to rely on each other for support.

School

Since the 1940s more than 700,000 American teenagers have attended high school overseas, in institutions with enrollments ranging from 10 students to nearly 6,000. A 1990 survey showed that there are 176 American schools scattered throughout 106 countries, teaching a total of more than 90,000 children, 24,000 of whom are American citizens.[8]

Children who attend international schools often have difficulties when they return to their passport country and enroll in the public school system. International schools tend to have small classes, reasonable student/teacher ratios, and well-motivated students. In addition, most of these schools place a strong emphasis on local language, history, and culture. Children educated in the international system often feel lost or disconnected when they enroll in domestic public schools because of large classes, staff shortages, cultural disparities, and relative anonymity:

> At my high school in Mexico City, I was somebody special. We were a close-knit group anyway, but because our school was so small, everybody knew everybody else. When my parents were transferred to Los Angeles, I enrolled in a school where my class population was larger than the population of our entire school in Mexico. I felt lost. I didn't know anybody, I didn't understand anybody, and I had trouble making friends.
>
> I eventually gravitated to the Chicano population in the school, and because of my Spanish language ability and cultural leanings I quickly became a part of their group. Beyond them, though, I was an outsider.

Because of the problems that many children encounter upon their return to public school, some companies—although they are far and away a minority—pay for private school for their returning employees' children. More commonly, multinational corporations offer private schooling to the children of employees who are third-country nationals, particularly those who have worked in multiple locations and have therefore had their children in several different schools.

The Five Cs

According to Norma McCaig, there are many forces that affect the ease with which children undergo reentry. Parents can lessen the impact on their children during the transition by following what she calls the Five Cs: communication, continuity, collaboration, closure, and cultural confirmation.

Communication

Talk to your children. Discuss the upcoming move as early as possible, and be honest with them about your own fears, excitement, and trepidation. Encourage them to talk freely about their own feelings. Be supportive, encouraging, and sensitive. Nothing is more important during this process than proper and complete preparation for the task of reentry. Try to prepare children for reentry by establishing a set of reasonable expectations prior to departure. Use the maxim "It won't be good or bad, just different" as a defining credo:

> As soon as we knew we were definitely going, I wrote to the Chamber of Commerce [in Ann Arbor] and told them that we would be moving there within the next few months. I also told them that I had grade-school kids, and asked them to send any information they had on life in the area.
>
> Well, they were great. They sent magazines, pictures, and school information, which I used as a guide for talks about the upcoming move. When we actually got there, the kids already knew what park they wanted to visit first. It was great.

Continuity

Reentry is often a disruptive and painful process for children. Try to minimize this disruption by maintaining as much continuity as possible in day-to-day family life. If the family has certain daily patterns that it follows in the host country, try to follow the same or similar patterns following repatriation. For young children, try to recreate their physical environment by hanging familiar pictures, using the same bedspread, scattering favorite toys:

> Our kids were still pretty young when we moved. Since I knew they'd have a hard time and probably wouldn't understand everything that was going on,

> I worked hard to maintain as much commonality between the two places [home and host country houses] as I could. I packed stuffed animals, pictures on the walls of their rooms, even favorite candy and cookies that I knew we wouldn't be able to get, and took them in our luggage. That allowed me to reconstruct their rooms pretty closely, and I think it helped.

Collaboration

Perhaps the hardest part of reentry (or of any move) for children is the sense that they have no control over the direction their lives are taking. To minimize this, involve children as much as possible in the planning process.

For example, if the family plans a vacation between leaving the host country and entering the new home (and this is highly recommended), let the children play a role in selecting the venue and daily activities. Let them decide which of their personal items they can keep with them during the move, and which are to be packed:

> When we transferred home, we planned a three-week vacation in the middle of the move. To keep the boys in the loop, we allowed them to plan the whole thing. Actually, we picked the destination as a family, but they got to research the place, plan our itinerary, and decide what we were going to do once we got there. It was kind of fun, and they felt that they were part of the move process.

Closure

In the same way that adults must consciously take the time to say good-bye when they leave the host country, children must be encouraged to do the same. Make sure that enough time is allotted for your children to have the time to say good-bye to friends. Encourage them to do so, even though it is painful and difficult. Mental health professionals who do research on repatriation anxiety conclude that failure *at any age* to say good-bye can lead to emotional stress that stays with a person for their entire life. *Say good-bye, and ensure that the children do, also.*

It is equally important to help children, especially younger children, make friends in the new locale. They should, however, be encouraged to maintain contact with the friends they left behind:

> Our kids' friendships with other children in Greece have been great for them. Besides the obvious value of friendship, their peers overseas have helped them get through the problems they've had trying to "become American kids" again. They're like the bridge between our kids' two worlds.

Cultural Confirmation

When children return to their passport country, they will be confronted with the reality of their multicultural identity. The issues discussed in this book will come to bear upon them, and they will need help to understand why they feel the way they do. This set of feelings, which I call expatriosis and is also known as reverse culture shock or repatriate syndrome, is perfectly normal, but not easy to weather.

During the reentry process it is critical that parents repeatedly affirm the tremendous value of their children's multicultural background. For this to work, parents must believe it *themselves*. They should take the time to talk to each other, to affirm their own beliefs, and to understand the changes that *they* will undergo upon reentry, prior to discussing the transition with their children:

> I moved to the United States from Germany when I was eleven, and I've been here now for a long time. Whenever I visit my relatives in Germany, they tell me I speak German with an accent and am obviously not German. Yet Americans always comment on my accent and ask me where I'm from. It's really irritating sometimes—I feel like I don't fit in anywhere. I'm old enough to appreciate my background now and the fact that I speak two languages, but my feelings got hurt a lot when I was a child.

Some companies offer counseling services for their returning employees as part of the formal reentry process. The counseling is provided either by specially trained human resources personnel or by outside professionals.[9]

Summary

The special needs of children are often overlooked in an overseas move, if for no other reason than that children may have difficulty expressing what they are feeling during the transition. The impact of an international move is as hard on children as it is on adults, so parents should take special care to explain to them what they should expect, prepare them properly for the move, help them with the transition abroad, and ensure that an adequate peer and school-based support structure gets established for them early on. For children, the experience of living overseas is immensely valuable and may not be repeated. Parents should do everything they can to ensure that it is a positive experience from the beginning.

Questions for Review

1. How can an employee and their family most effectively manage and balance the various impacts of the "Spheres of Influence" shown on page 139? How can the employee help their family manage the influences shown on page 136?

2. Describe the five stages the global nomad goes through. How can a parent or teacher recognize each phase?

3. In addition to those discussed in the text, what items should parents take with them to help children with their overseas transitions?

4. What role can teachers play to ease transition difficulties for children?

5. Why is reentry often perceived to be harder on teens than on any other age group?

Notes

1. From R. H. Useem and R. D. Downie, "Third Culture Kids," *Today's Education,* September-October 1976, pp. 103–105.

2. *Third culture kids,* or *TCKs,* is a term coined by Dr. Useem. Other organizations, such as Global Nomads International, refer to these children as global nomads. The term *third culture kids* recognizes that the children are from neither their parents' culture nor the culture(s) in which they grew up, but rather from some combination of the two—hence, the third culture.

3. Cited in *Global Nomads Newsletter,* Fall 1993.

4. S. L. Werkman and F. Johnson, *The Effect of Geographic Mobility on Adolescent Character Structure.* Paper presented at the annual meeting of the American Society for Adolescent Psychiatry, Miami, Florida, May 1976.

5. Reprinted by permission from *Global Nomads Newsletter,* Fall 1993.

6. If you are interested in learning more through articles, tapes, books, videos, workshops or small groups, call Global Nomads International at (703) 993-2975, or send e-mail to info@gni.org. Much information is available, and fascinating research is going on at several universities around the country.

7. Published by the Overseas Briefing Center, Foreign Service Institute, U.S. Department of State.

8. Carolyn D. Smith, *The Absentee American* (Bayside, NY: Aletheia Publications, 1994), pp. 3–4.

9. Please refer to the Organization List in the Appendix for additional information about these organizations.

7

Creating a Multinational Employee Management Strategy

> *Objectives are not fate; they are direction. They are not commands; they are commitments. They do not determine the future; they are means to mobilize the resources and energies of the business for the making of the future.*
>
> Peter F. Drucker,
> *People and Performance*

As corporations expand into global markets, the number of expatriates—and therefore returning expatriates—grows faster than ever before. With the proliferation of international trade pacts such as the North American Free Trade Agreement (NAFTA), the World Trade Organization (WTO), and the European Community (EC), multinational corporations are fast becoming the rule rather than the exception. They aren't just U.S. corporations, either: A study conducted in 1994 by the University of Pennsylvania's Wharton School of Business found that over 2 million Americans worked for foreign corporations in 1991.[1]

The preceding sections of this book examined the issues that expatriates face while working abroad and the difficulties they encounter when they return to the domestic organization. While it is expensive to post employees overseas, improved access to new markets makes the expense a valid cost of doing business.

As these employees return from their overseas assignments, they bring with them valuable skills and knowledge. If they don't already, these employees will soon constitute a sizable proportion of the overall employee pool. They must be nurtured, cultivated, and recognized as important corporate contributors.

In the same way that employees have a responsibility to the corporation to perform their jobs to the best of their ability, the corporation has a responsibility to the employees—and to itself—to safeguard its valuable human resources. The creation and support of an aggressive, proactive strategy for the management of expatriate employee affairs can bridge the gap between domestic and expatriate workforces and eliminate the very real problems of culture shock and reverse culture shock.

Human resources executives traditionally cite three key factors that cause difficulties for expatriates. The first is the corporation's rationale for sending employees off to foreign assignments in the first place. In most cases employees are assigned to overseas positions either because they are being positioned for senior management assignments or because they offer a specialized skill that is required but not available in the host country. These are not the only reasons, however. In far too many companies, less than optimal performers are sent overseas to staff fledgling organizations that are hungry for personnel. While this practice solves the short-term local problem of what to do with poor performers, it creates bigger problems elsewhere. These people represent the corporation in a potentially lucrative market and are not the best choice for a minimally supervised assignment that will undoubtedly require sophisticated social, diplomatic, and managerial skills.

Also, they eventually return home. If their skills are substandard to begin with, they will not improve during the stint abroad. The problem of marginally competent employees is not unique to the international workforce. It is a fundamental management problem that must be dealt with, not avoided by sending the employee abroad.

Another practice that has developed recently is the trend to shift employees to overseas positions as a way to meet corporate downsizing objectives. Again, this may resolve a short-term problem, but in the long run it may not be strategically beneficial.

The second cause of expatriate difficulties is professional disposition of the returning employee, who arrives with an enhanced set of skills that can be valuable if applied properly. For example, an employee returning from an assignment in Latin America could be useful to a domestic organization involved in business pursuits in that same region. Such an employee can draw on their experience abroad to provide the corporation with insights about language, culture, business practices, economic and social trends, local competition, and other information that would not otherwise be available. Some of that information is available in the form of country-specific intelligence reports, but there is no substitute for firsthand knowledge provided by an in-country resource. In many cases, however, the organization that the employee returns to is a domestic business unit that has no use for and little understanding of the enhanced capabilities of the newly arrived employee.

Finally, there is reverse culture shock. Many companies believe that the move abroad is the most difficult part of an international assignment. In fact, however, the return home can be far more difficult. When families come "home" following an extended international assignment, they often do not return to the same home, friends, social circles, or even town: They start over. If the returning expatriates are allowed to believe that they are returning to the life they left behind, they are in for a rude awakening. For them the passport country is, in many ways, just another foreign assignment, albeit a permanent or semipermanent one.

These three factors—selection for an overseas assignment, professional disposition following return to the passport country, and reverse culture shock—can be managed effectively, and that can mean the difference between success and failure in a cross-cultural assignment.

Corporations must create a preparation and training environment that does as good a job repatriating employees as it does expatriating them. Many companies, for example, make language training available to employees bound for overseas posts, as well as cross-cultural training and seminars on foreign business practices. These are all deemed to be good investments because they prepare the employee for a task that is complicated by the need to operate in a different culture and thus enhance their chances of success in the overseas position.

But what about the same employee who returns home after several years abroad? Are not the cultural differences just as significant? In fact, they are. Many expatriates return to find that the argot of everyday speech has changed enough to make many of the words they remember obsolete. In some cases, the expatriate will have picked up commonly used terms within the expatriate community in the host country that have no meaning, or the wrong meaning, in their passport country:

> I really had some catching up to do when I came home from London. Not only did I use words for common things that no one understood—the "boot" for a car trunk, "bonnet" for the hood, that sort of thing—but I also used a lot of idiomatic expressions and word pronunciations that had no meaning in the U.S. I spent a lot of time with a red face, because some of the innocuous expressions I used in England have pretty colorful meanings in the States!

And what of business practices? Have corporate goals changed, or has the focus shifted in some intangible way that would be perceptible only to those who are steeped in it every day? By the same token, what mechanisms are available to help the expatriate and their family with the difficult task of integration back into their home country lifestyle? *Can* they rejoin that lifestyle? Without assistance, the process can be formidable:

> Talk about feeling lost. I knew everything I thought I needed to know when I came back, because I read all the e-mail, talked to friends, stayed abreast of changes in the org chart, all those sorts of things. But what I *didn't* have, because there was no way I *could* have, was a sense of the changes in the corporate culture. Like who's now perceived to be the

leader in each organization, who's in and out of favor, how people are feeling about the company, the kinds of things that you can only get a sense of by being there, day after day. I'm a pretty perceptive person, and I've been with this company for almost twenty years, but it took me a good three months to get tuned back in to the point that I felt like I really knew what was going on. It was tough.

There are many valuable resources that the corporation can use to this end. One of the best is the cadre of former expatriates who now work for the corporation in domestic positions. Some corporations create teams of "ex-expatriates" who help returning employees go through the initial transition period. Similarly, their family members are often pressed into service to help spouses and children deal with the rocky shoals of reentry. The mentor can help guide this phase of transitional activity:

> We moved to San Francisco after four years in Madrid. Luckily, San Francisco is the headquarters location for my father's company, and as it turned out, several families we had known in Spain now lived there as well. So I had instant friends who also understood what I was going through during reentry.

These suggestions and the guidelines that follow can be used to create an effective management strategy for expatriate employees.

Issues, Concerns, and Special Cases

The challenges addressed in the preceding section are typical of most international assignments. However, there are a number of special case issues that, because of their unique impact, will be addressed below. These include the problems of interorganizational transfers, home office education, peer counseling and family support, tangible and intangible compensation issues, foreign business practices, the unique role of the multinational manager, the special cases of technical employees, foreign nationals, the expatriate employee's unique fiscal responsibilities, and short-term assignments.

Interorganizational Transfers

In some corporations, appointment to an overseas position means a transfer to the international division, which may be distinct from the employee's original, domestic division. If the employee anticipates that they will return to the same corporation, the mentor should ensure that the employee is kept on both formal and informal organizational distribution lists from both the international and domestic organizations.

This can be particularly important when issues of job security surface. Today's corporation is enormously dynamic, and employees often feel seriously disadvantaged if they are not kept aware of human resources decisions that might affect them. This is particularly true when complicated by distance.

Employees often develop an "exile complex" that stems from anxiety over whether they have been forgotten back home. It is therefore not only prudent but critical to keep expatriate employees in the domestic corporate information loop.

As telecommunications technologies advance and video-based applications become less expensive, regularly scheduled video teleconferences or traditional conference calls can be conducted to help maintain the psychic and emotional link to home. Many corporations are already using these techniques to conduct meetings; while expensive, they are far less costly than flying employees home for the meeting.

In at least one company, Internet relay chat (IRC) servers are used by employees in several countries to conduct "conference calls" over the Internet. This allows overseas and domestic employees to stay in touch with one another on an informal, ad hoc basis at comparatively little cost.

This use of communications technology to improve corporate communications is a growing trend in modern corporations. E-mail, IRC, the World Wide Web, and Internet telephony are all helping to make the distances between domestic and overseas employees "go away."

Turnabout: Educate the Home Office

While it is important to keep the expatriate informed of domestic corporate activities, the converse is also true. Goings-on in the overseas organization are often a mystery to domestic employees, especially in large corporations or corporations that have geographically dispersed subsidiaries. The overseas division should take on the responsibility of educating the domestic division to help reduce the sense of difference between the two. This educational process can be conducted by expatriate employees and facilitated by their mentors.

> The line managers in our [Pacific Rim] organization got together with their peers at headquarters during one of their quarterly status meetings and put together a "show and tell" for each other that described what the hot issues were in each organization, the status of the business in each region, and so on. It generated so much interest and so many questions that they decided to make it a regular thing, and eventually made it available to the entire company by posting it on the Web server. We've now made that a requirement for all of our overseas divisions. Not only does it help the domestic and overseas organizations understand each other, it's also proven to be a good tool for people who are about to transfer overseas or back home again.

Some companies require expatriates to draft a regularly published report that covers business activities in the foreign post; this is distributed throughout the domestic organization. Alternatively, the overseas employee might be invited to conduct presentations for the domestic organization on an annual or semiannual basis. These would be designed to familiarize staff with international corporate activities, but they also have a secondary benefit: They acquaint the employee with the domestic organization and vice versa:

> One of Roger's objectives was to publish a quarterly report that told everybody at home what was going on while he was in Singapore. It was required reading for everybody in the group, and after a few months people actually started to get interested (probably more because he interjected all sorts of odd cultural things in addition to the business report).
>
> Anyway, when he came home, I handed out two assignments. One was to Roger, in which he had to design the ideal domestic job for himself in the group; the other was to everybody else in the group, with instructions to state how we could best use Roger's abilities. They looked like they were written by the same person. And while we didn't create that exact position, we *did* create something that was close—probably a lot closer than he would have come home to otherwise.

In organizations that experience employee turnover due to rotation through international assignments, domestic divisions should be encouraged to undergo "sensitivity training" to prepare them to deal with returned expatriates. This can be as simple as a presentation on the issues discussed in this book or on the specific activities the expatriate has been involved in during their time abroad.

Putting the Skills to Work

The best way to take advantage of the skills of returned expatriates is to recognize that they can contribute at three functional levels: operational, tactical, and strategic. To determine the best fit with the employee's newfound skills, the mentor or the employee's domestic supervisor should take into account three things: the length of time the employee was overseas; the nature of their position while there; and the employee's level within the company.

Operational Skills

Operational skills are those that are required for the day-to-day functions of the business unit, regardless of whether it is located overseas or in the home country. These include office operations, routine customer interface issues, local labor practices, and ordinances that affect work practices. When the expatriate returns to the domestic organization from an overseas position, their knowledge about these practical matters can be valuable. These issues are most typically faced and dealt with by transient personnel such as technical support and implementation staff and sales and marketing employees.

Motorola takes advantage of these skills as a matter of course. The nature of their business requires technical employees (engineers, for the most part) to travel extensively, often remaining in the host country for months at a time while they provide technical support to customers. During their sojourn abroad these engineers amass significant amounts of local operational intelligence, which becomes important to other engineers and support personnel. The information is shared primarily via e-mail and face-to-face encounters, although some staff members have created internal Web sites (Intranets) where the information can be archived for access by anyone in the organization. These databases include such routine (but important) data as locations of equipment sites, local ordinances that affect work practices, and contact personnel for access to buildings and equipment closets. While these may seem prosaic, they are immense time-savers for in-country personnel and add greatly to the professional image that the company presents to its clients.

Hill Associates is an international telecommunications education company with offices in the United States and Australia. When instructors and office management staff return from overseas assignments, they are required to meet with headquarters management staff shortly after they arrive. At the meeting they brief management about the technical evolution of the student population; training center logistics and staff changes; and cultural, political, and business issues that might have an impact on outbound instructors, sales and marketing personnel, course developers, and travel planners. They also address the appropriateness and accuracy of instructional materials. They use e-mail and the World Wide Web extensively to send regular status reports and news announcements to the home office and to expatriates. This not only keeps headquarters staff informed about goings-on in Australia but also provides a feedback loop for the overseas employee. "It also helps to keep phone bills reasonable," says Mark Fei, a senior member of technical staff at Hill and co-manager of the company's office in Melbourne.

> It gets lonely down here, and it's pretty easy to feel isolated. It's way too expensive to pick up the phone and call [the headquarters in] Vermont every day, so we use e-mail. I can dial a local number in Sydney, Melbourne, Perth, or wherever I happen to be, get into the Internet, and download mail for the cost of a local phone call. That way I stay connected to my friends back in the Colchester [Vermont] and Denver offices, and stay tuned in to what's going on. I don't feel so isolated that way.

Tactical Skills

Tactical skills are those that have a more long-term focus than operational issues, but not as long as those that are strategic in nature. They tend to have a one- to six-month horizon, in the sense that they will generally be executed or have their impact felt within that time frame. These include such issues as imminent local political changes, impending changes in tax law, and labor activities that may surface in the foreseeable future. These issues typically confront office managers, in-country human resources and accounting personnel, or labor relations staff:

When I came home from Croatia, I made it a point to sit down with the manager who replaced me to fill him in on all the things that were under way. But it was more important that I fill him in on the things that weren't yet under way, but that would be not long after he got there.

I also sat down with the folks in the domestic accounting groups and with labor relations to fill them in on some things that we felt were coming and that would affect our operation over there. For example, they didn't know that the relationship we had with the BOAL [a local union] was changing—not in a bad way, but certainly in a way that they would need to know about. We also had learned some things about Croatian negotiation practices that no one realized. There was a guy who was their primary negotiator, and he had a very effective tactic that he used to intimidate the people he was negotiating with. He would pretend to get frustrated, then extremely angry. Then he would shatter his glasses on the tabletop and stalk out of the room, knowing that his act would unnerve the others so badly that they would often bow to his demands. Well, we saw him do this a few times, and figured out that it was a carefully planned tactic. We quit letting it bother us, and it took the wind out of his sails. Well, there was no way that the domestic folks could know about that. So our intelligence was pretty important to the home office.

Strategic Skills

Strategic skills are perhaps the hardest to assess, report, and act upon. They are defined as those skills that affect the outcome of a long-term corporate objective, and are normally part of the skill set of middle and senior management personnel. Their strategic focus is generally projected well into the future and is concerned with profitability, long-term customer and alliance/partner relationships, and product viability within the markets they manage. The input of strategic planners is of crucial significance, therefore, to senior decision-makers in the domestic organization. When overseas employers who manage at strategic levels return to the domestic organization, they should be asked for their input:

> There are markets emerging down there [in South America] that we don't have a clue about because we're not down there. Even the marketing folks and country managers who conscientiously visit down there on a regular basis aren't tuned in enough, because the only way to see what amounts to a slow "sea change" in the market is to be there, every day, day in and day out, and actually be part of the change. The only people who see it are our people who live down there for a few years and manage to get their arms around the market. So not only do I want regular reports from them while they're over there, I want to pick their brains when they come home. In fact, I want them to become

an available resource to the people who replace them and the groups here [in the domestic office] that respond to the input from the folks overseas. If I were a spy, I'd call them intelligence moles, but friendly ones.

When these employees return from their overseas assignments, part of their repatriation program should be a two-part intelligence-gathering process. The first part should be initiated by the company and should have several goals: first, to assess the extent and nature of the employee's operational, tactical, and strategic knowledge; second, to determine what people or organizations could best and most immediately benefit from the employee's knowledge; and third, to design a position for the employee that takes best advantage of their skills. This helps cement the relationship between the employee and the company by empowering the employee and providing a source of highly useful intelligence for the corporation.

The second part of the process should be aggressively initiated by the employee, who must prove their value to the company in ways that go beyond what they had to offer prior to their overseas experience. Employees should schedule a meeting to share their knowledge with managers who are at the appropriate level to benefit from their input. This action has two benefits. First, it positions the employee as an expert; second, and perhaps more important, it increases the employee's visibility in the domestic organization:

I don't recommend what I did to everyone, but it worked for me. When I came home from Malaysia, I put together a presentation about my experiences. And it wasn't just a "Jack's excellent adventures in Kuala Lumpur" thing: I looked at country cultural issues, business practices, emerging markets, pitfalls that I felt would bite us somewhere down the road if we're not careful, and a list of things that I felt needed to change in the way we're doing business over there if we're going to be successful in the long term. I also wrote a white paper to accompany the presentation and sent the paper to the chairman of the board, asking him for an audience to discuss what I felt were strategically important issues that had to do with our success in Asia. Well, I didn't get an audience with Stewart [the CEO], but I did get a meeting with the EVP of marketing. He read my paper, then scheduled a meeting with all of his staff for my talk. Part of my white paper was a suggested position for myself, and by the end of the session I had it. I'm now the market liaison person for Asia operations, and my job is to stay in touch with the in-country managers and feed information back to senior management about the state of affairs in the region.

None of this would have happened if I hadn't taken the bull by the horns and established myself as an expert before I got pigeonholed in a cubicle somewhere. The good news is that that was four years ago, and I'm still here.

Peer Counseling and Family Support

One way to ease the impact of cross-cultural transition is to arrange for family support administered by "seasoned troops" who have been in the host country for awhile or have been home for some time and have already dealt with the rigors of culture shock.

Most companies arrange for new expatriates to be met by their overseas peers, who then guide them through the first few weeks or months of life in the expatriate community. While these programs are informal, they are effective.

Both AT&T and Coca-Cola Corporation, for example, provide readjustment activities that employees and their families are required to take part in (see case study, page 75). These sessions are conducted by trained industrial psychologists who are familiar with reentry difficulties. A variety of reentry awareness seminars are conducted that are targeted specifically at employees, their spouses, and their children. Many companies also provide an opportunity for newly returned employees to talk to former expatriates who have been home for some time. They schedule formal "welcome home" gatherings that are attended by both the new arrivals and a cadre of former expatriates who have been back for awhile.

Similarly, many European companies train and employ executive mentors instead of professional counselors. They contend that at a professional level these internal managers are better equipped to help the employee readjust, since they are familiar with corporate operations, politics, and policy.

It should be the responsibility of the mentor to schedule reentry "training" for the employee and their family. Ideally, the training begins before they actually come home. The Peace Corps, which repatriates over 4,000 people every year, holds a Close of Service Conference for returnees three months before their actual return. These conferences are designed to facilitate the reintroduction of returning Peace Corps volunteers (RPCVs) into U.S. society and the workplace. A wide array of subjects are addressed during these conferences, including a review of each volunteer's experiences abroad and the lessons they learned during their time in-country; a look to the future, with career and professional placement in mind; and an exploration of personal and professional options.

Consultants for International Living (see page 111) conducts Journey Home Workshops, which are held in the host country and conducted within a year prior to repatriation.

Compensation Issues

> When we transferred to Spain from west Texas in 1969, we naturally took with us a set of domestic values that dictated the nature of the home environment in which we wanted to raise our family.
>
> Madrid is an apartment city. There are very few houses, and those that are available are typically rather large. Because we had always lived in a house, and because we had three rambunctious

boys, we wanted a place with a yard. It took us nearly six months to find a house to rent; as foreign aliens, we weren't allowed to purchase, nor was it recommended. While there was little chance of it in Spain at the time, it is often inadvisable to invest in foreign real estate because of the danger of currency devaluation.

When we finally found a house, it was big. It had nine bedrooms, six bathrooms, three kitchens, a dining room that could do double duty as a ballroom, a central courtyard, a huge back yard, a pool, a library, a rumpus room in the basement, servants' quarters, and of course, servants. Needless to say, this was just a tad different from what we had known in Texas, but in the strictest sense of the word, it was a house—and that's what we wanted. You can imagine what we went through when, in 1974, we were transferred to California, where an affordable mortgage bought us a house, but nothing even close to the home we had become accustomed to in Spain.

This situation is not unique. It afflicts many returned expatriates, and the reactions range from mild annoyance to severe depression. While this reaction may appear overly materialistic to those who have not experienced it, the disparity in "living conditions" between two countries can be quite dramatic and the transitional shock equally so.

By the same token, salary disparities must be clearly articulated and understood by both the company and the employee prior to departure. Many companies offer their expatriate employees a premium salary as an incentive to go overseas. Typically, it is paid as either an add-on to the monthly paycheck; a one-time "balloon payment" when the employee actually moves overseas; as two payments, one paid on departure, the other on return; or as a lump sum, paid when the employee returns.

Some overseas positions provide additional compensation because of difficult living conditions, cost-of-living disparities, or an unstable political environment. This is sometimes referred to as "hardship pay," "hazard pay," or "swamp pay." This becomes more of a concern when the dollar is weak against other currencies, which reduces the buying power of U.S. expatriates' salaries.

Expatriates often learn to live on significantly less than they actually earn while overseas. As a result, they either bank a considerable amount of their salary or enjoy large amounts of disposable income. This is both a blessing and a curse.

Some expatriates are financially informed enough to understand that the additional income they receive while overseas is temporary. They don't allow their expenses to rise to the point that they depend on that money: They bank the additional income and return home with a sizable nest egg salted away.

Others, however, react differently, allowing their expenses to follow Parkinson's Law,[2] expanding to exceed their actual income. When the time comes to return home, they often experience "sticker shock" when the additional income that came with the overseas assignment evaporates and they have nothing to show financially for the time spent abroad.

Unfortunately, this reaction is extremely common. Prior to the start of an overseas assignment the corporation should counsel the employee and their family about the financial and social issues associated with an overseas assignment. The purpose of the additional income should be very clearly stated.

As obvious as it may appear, the employee must be told in very clear terms that the additional income will appear on the paycheck only for the duration of the overseas assignment. Some companies employ financial advisors to assist expatriates with these issues. If the corporation uses a letter of understanding between the company and the employee, compensation details should be clearly and completely documented in it.

The issue of additional pay for acceptance of a hardship post can cause problems from a slightly different direction as well. As discussed earlier, some employees, recognized as having potential for movement to higher levels of management, are given international assignments as part of a training or assessment process. More than once, companies have seen this strategy backfire when the international manager finds the overseas assignment more lucrative than the one to which they will return at the end of their tour. Not only does this create friction between the company and the employee over salary matters, it may create problems for the company when it is ready to repatriate the employee for a domestic assignment—an assignment the employee may not want.

It is critical that the returning employee's salary treatment be carefully managed by the corporation. Failure to do so can result in a disgruntled employee who will leave at the first opportunity.

A corporation's expatriate compensation program should be designed to accomplish the following:

- Attract and keep employees who want to work overseas and are qualified for an international assignment.

- Maintain and clearly state a reasonable relationship between the salaries of domestic employees and those stationed abroad. Create a clearly written expatriate compensation plan that details all compensation components. If letters of understanding are employed, compensation details should be documented in them.

- If there are numerous international locations, compensation levels at all locations should be reasonably similar in order to prevent "salary shock" when employees move from post to post.

- If appropriate, provide financial assistance for employees returning to the passport country.

Intangible Components of Compensation

Sometimes additional compensation comes in nonmonetary forms. In some countries the social environment dictates that club memberships, typically very expensive, are a necessary part of life because business is often transacted in clubs. Many companies pay for these memberships as well as providing cost-of-living assistance such as subsidized housing, local tax protection, company cars and drivers, fuel, and domestic help.

In addition to the financial shock that accompanies the return home, there is often a jarring social shock. The sixteen-room mansion is gone, replaced by an ordinary house; the free car and chauffeur have driven off into the sunset; the club membership is just a memory; and the maids, cooks, and gardeners are left behind.

In *Video Night in Kathmandu and Other Reports from the Not-So-Far-East,* author Pico Iyer listens to an expatriate resident of Hong Kong as he explains the trap of expatriate life:

> I know this Welsh architect. He left a dull job in some grimy town and came over here. Suddenly he had maids, cars, an oceanfront villa in Repulse Bay. The firm paid for his children's schooling and for his private clubs. When his time was up, after 36 months, he was willing to do anything—anything at all—to extend his stay. Anything. He was almost begging.

Do not underestimate the need for clear, ongoing dialogue about individual components of compensation. Employees must understand their compensation package prior to departing for the foreign post, and as their time in-country lengthens, they should receive regular status reports. During their stay abroad and particularly when repatriation time nears, the corporation (usually in the form of the employee's manager or mentor) should ensure that the employee receives financial counseling and has available to them financial advisors to help plan for the transition.

Foreign Business Practices

Jeffrey Wade[3] works for a multinational corporation that manufactures farm equipment. Recently he was sent to a Latin American country to expand the company's market there, his first international assignment:

> Shortly after my arrival, I met with a government minister, who made it clear that my company's chances of success would be improved if we were to pay what amounted to a bribe to the official. There was nothing secretive about the official's behavior, either; the request was made as plainly as one might order dinner in a restaurant. In fact, it was over dinner in a restaurant—somewhere between the drinks and the hors d'oeuvres.
>
> Needless to say, I was shocked at this blatant display of obviously illegal behavior. I fumbled about and muttered my way out of the meeting, clearly at a loss as to the proper response to the minister.

(Continued on p. 184)

> To the public opinion
>
> The workers of catering Entursa (supriver of foof to the air craft) are in strike since O.O.h. of 25 h. The motives are: the direccion uncompromising, in aplicate the wages revision, it was recoguire in the valid agreement making deaf hears to this establishment.
>
> The enterprise cowmittee and the workers after finish all the ways to their reach to come in agreement, they are in assambly to do the only thing they can do: the strike
>
> The enterprise once the strike has begin, the don't want to know anything abant the regulations. They don't let the us to go inside the instalacions.
>
> In the presence of a new contac, to negociate with the enterprise, as answer they say the know our good organitation—and we can go to work.
>
> As you see they don't change their attitude this leaf and oltros we want to send you, if for you to know our problem and you to jamat with us
>
> The strike committee

Expatriate managers often have to deal with surprises, such as this Croatian strike announcement. How would you respond?

Unfortunately, this kind of behavior is a fact of life in many countries, and is not necessarily illegal under their laws. From Wade's purely ethnocentric perspective, the official was corrupt. From the other side of the fence, though, things look different. Government officials in many countries are severely underpaid and operate in bureaucracies that are slow and ineffective. Their ability to carry out their jobs is severely hampered, so they do business in the most effective way they know.

For U.S. expatriates, the Foreign Corrupt Practices Act specifically prohibits business activities in other countries that would be illegal in the United States, effective though these practices may be. Prohibited or not, the expatriate employee may be faced with similar ethical quandaries that involve enormous responsibility and have far-reaching implications.

Multinational corporations must prepare their expatriates to face these sorts of intangible challenges. With experience, most find ways to solve such problems in completely legal—and honorable—ways. When faced with a moral quandary, some companies, such as the one just described, simply put the local representative on their own staff as an advisor or business consultant and pay them a reasonable salary for their services. In other cases expatriate corporations may donate money to local educational institutions or contribute in some way to the development of local infrastructure such as road building, refinery construction, or school campus improvement.

These innovative approaches to seemingly insurmountable problems rapidly become a way of life for the expatriate employee. For example, in 1981 Bob and Gloria Shepard (the author's parents) were transferred to Zagreb, Yugoslavia. Shepard, now retired, was the managing director for a large multinational oil company. Because Yugoslavia was an eastern bloc country, the labor practices he had to deal with were quite different from those he was familiar with at home. Like many multinational corporations, Shepard's company formed a joint venture with the Yugoslav national oil company. Most of the employees were Yugoslavs, and the management practices were those of that society. For example, if an employee was to be reprimanded for some work-related infraction, the entire pool of company employees, called the Basic Organization of Associated Labor (BOAL), had to be convened in a large meeting room to listen to management's concerns and then debate the employee's fate. The infraction was not between the employer and the employee; it involved all the employees. A simple discussion and verbal reprimand that could have taken five minutes often stretched into weeks, during which very little productive work was accomplished. The responsibility of managing in such an environment is significantly greater and more challenging than in a familiar domestic context.

Similarly, families become adept at the skills necessary for "psychic survival" in a foreign culture. They learn to bend with the cultural nuances that define life in a different country, and adapt to them in order to fit in and make friends:

Every Monday and Wednesday morning, I would get up early and walk down to the little pastry shop in town, stopping first at the flower lady's stand on the corner. I'd always buy a bunch of daisies and take them to the lady that ran the pastry shop, because I knew that she loved flowers and that she appreciated the effort. In return, she always took care of me, setting aside special things for me and the kids. Call it bribery, if you want; I call it getting into the local culture.

My Mom, who was the quietest, kindest, most demure lady you've ever seen, became a different person when she went shopping. She knew that if she didn't get in there and yell and push like everybody else, she'd be left holding an empty bag. It didn't take her long to get into the swing of things. And as soon as she had what she wanted, she turned back into Mom again. It was pretty funny.

Fiscal Responsibilities of the Expatriate Employee

Expatriate employees often have broader fiscal responsibilities than their domestic counterparts. Because of the logistics associated with doing business internationally, purchases that would normally require approval by several layers of management in the domestic organization often must be assessed and made immediately and independently by the resident manager. Consequently, expatriates become adept at making effective, independent economic decisions.

(Continued on p. 188)

A Special Case:
The Technical Employee

The increasingly technical nature of the workplace has led to a growing demand for highly specialized personnel. This is magnified in the multinational environment, where the level of technological development is often very different in the passport and host countries. This leads to an increased need for personnel in overseas positions to handle specific tasks, sometimes referred to as "firefighting roles."

Technical employees rely on highly specific knowledge and skills to perform their jobs. This knowledge is accumulated from a variety of sources, including technical journals, trade shows, training seminars, hands-on experience, and direct interaction with peers. When these employees are placed in foreign assignments, their exposure to sources of current technical information is often severely limited. This can lead to an erosion of the employee's existing knowledge base and can have an impact on technical currency.

This loss of capability and currency can have serious career implications. One employee who was interviewed during the preparation of this book was told flatly upon his return from an assignment in Europe that because of the time he had spent abroad, he was no longer qualified to perform the job he had left when he went overseas, much less something more complex. For this employee, the overseas assignment had a profoundly negative impact.

> Technically skilled employees are clearly necessary for international operations. If the employee's destination country is one that will not provide the technical environment required to maintain expertise, the sending agency should take steps to prevent "intellectual erosion." These might include easy access to electronic sources of information, such as corporate e-mail or the World Wide Web; scheduled in-country seminars; or mandatory trips home so that the employee can take advantage of training opportunities and mingle with peers. This ongoing process can be effectively facilitated by the mentor.

When these employees return home, they are typically faced with smaller budgets to manage, more mundane responsibilities, and comparatively curtailed day-to-day responsibilities. They often feel bored, underutilized, and untrusted.

According to Douglas Martin, home office director of franchising for McDonald's International, this is one of the greatest professional challenges for returning expatriates:

> After working overseas for an extended period of time, our managers tend to become self-reliant, and capable of making tough, quick business decisions that involve significant amounts of money. We expect that of them. Unfortunately, when they return to the corporate fold, they often find themselves in jobs where their ability and authority to make decisions are curtailed—not because they
>
> *(Continued on p. 190)*

A Special Case:
The Short-Term Assignment

Occasionally employees are sent abroad for relatively short-term assignments. Many of these, because of the abbreviated length and high intensity of the employee's responsibilities while in-country, will not require much interaction with the local people, language, or culture. Others, however, require a significant amount of interaction, which means that the employee would be wise to arrive in the country armed with a reasonable amount of cultural familiarity. Expatriates whose jobs require these kinds of brief (but intense) country visits universally recommend the following actions prior to departure:

- Listen to short-wave radio broadcasts from the destination country.

- Locate and read local and foreign editions of newspapers in the destination country. "Even if you don't understand the language, you'll get a lot out of the layout and photographs."

- Talk to local residents and expatriates who have prior in-country experience.

- Call the country's embassy or consulate and ask them to send you a visitor's packet. Most consular offices have them prepared in advance for distribution.

- Read formal, country-specific publications, such as books from the Intercultural Press, Culturgrams from the David M. Kennedy Center for International Studies, the Price Waterhouse "Doing Business in [Country Name]" series, and Craighead Country Reports.

Sometimes a simple newspaper can be the best source of information:

> When I went to Australia to teach a class for three weeks, the smartest thing I did was read the Sydney newspaper for about a month before I went over there. By the time I got to the country, I knew a lot about the local culture and political goings-on, who the favorite sports teams were, what special dialect and jargon "gotchas" I needed to be familiar with, and even what things cost. When the time came, I really felt ready to go.

aren't capable of handling the decisions, but because the decision-making structure is different—more compartmentalized—at corporate. As a result, they often become frustrated. One of my greatest challenges is to bring those people back at the end of their tour and find satisfying "homes" for them.

Expatriate employees return from their overseas assignments with unique and valuable skills. If those skills are not recognized and used, employees grow restless and frustrated, and if the situation is

(Continued on p. 192)

Resource:
Craighead Country Reports

Craighead Country Reports are published for eighty different countries and provide comprehensive, country-specific information for people who travel and relocate overseas. They are a primary source of information for managers responsible for preparing their corporation's personnel for international assignments. According to the corporate information booklet,

> the country reports provide information necessary to understand and evaluate the political, economic, and business environment and everyday living conditions of foreign destinations. Important topics include a general country orientation; an economic and political overview; money, banking, and tax matters; business customs and protocol for meetings and entertainment; health and safety concerns; predeparture regulations; visas and work permits; "settling-in" issues; residential areas; typical housing; international schools; social etiquette and clubs; and costs of goods and services, schools, and housing, among other subjects.

See the Appendix for additional information about Craighead Country Reports.

> **Resource:**
> **Price Waterhouse**
> *Doing Business in [Country Name]*
>
> Price Waterhouse publishes a series of guidebooks targeted at international business travelers. The books are updated regularly and cover business practices in more than 100 countries, including culture and history, the local investment climate, generally accepted business rules, and accounting and taxation guidelines.
> For more information about Price Waterhouse, see the Appendix.

allowed to go on for too long they may take their skills elsewhere. A corporation that is sensitive to cross-cultural issues can forestall this "intellectual hemorrhage" by taking steps to find the right position for the returned employee. This requires an understanding of the employee's skills, a plan for taking advantage of them in the domestic organization, and an appreciation for the environment in which the employee worked during their time abroad.

Expatriation and repatriation processes should be closely aligned. Both should recognize that the affected individuals are important members of the business or social environment, whether they are beginning an international assignment or returning from one. Either way, there are bound to be difficulties. The forward-thinking corporation will have spent considerable time and energy to design a program that takes into account every possible expatriation and repatriation contingency.

Feedback

Any program that has a direct impact on employees must include an evaluation system to ensure that it accomplishes its goals. Some companies require that expatriate employees submit regular reports that detail the effectiveness of the program, or fill out periodic measurement surveys. Others require that employees write a "white paper" as their first official assignment following repatriation; the paper describes both the good and bad aspects of their overseas experience.

These tools are effective only if someone in the organization reads and uses the information they yield to improve the processes of expatriation and repatriation. Corporate mentors, working with human resources personnel, should establish a formal process to review and act upon the information submitted by current and former expatriate employees and their families.

Hill Associates, mentioned earlier, is a telecommunications education and consulting firm located in Colchester, Vermont. Its customer base has traditionally been domestic, but since 1996 it has had a growing presence in the Asia Pacific region and has opened an office in Melbourne to serve its customers in that part of the world. Because of the need to staff the Australia office, and because of the growing number of instructors who spend extended periods of time

> **Resource:**
> **Culturgrams**
> Culturgrams are published by the David M. Kennedy Center for International Studies at Brigham Young University. Each Culturgram is four pages long and consists of clear, concise information about the daily lives of the people who live in each country covered. Currently more than 150 Culturgrams are available, and new countries are added on a regular basis. Culturgrams are updated annually and can be purchased individually, grouped by region, or as a complete set.
>
> The Kennedy Center also publishes Infograms, which are briefings on select international and intercultural topics such as travel and international law, travel stress, expatriate family issues, and repatriation issues.
>
> See the Appendix for additional information about Culturgrams.

outside the United States, Hill Associates created an expatriate management program. "Since 1981, our domestic business has been based on travelers going to far-flung places to teach, so we're pretty good at managing people while they're on the road," says Linda Cook, vice president of human resources development at Hill. "But when the international business started to grow, we realized that this was a whole new ball game, and that we would have to do some things differently. We talked to companies that had experience with overseas employees and took

(Continued on p. 199)

A Special Case:
Foreign Nationals

Because of joint ventures, alliances, or other agreements with foreign business partners, many multinational corporations employ foreign nationals in domestic positions. IBM, for example, has manufacturing and intellectual property alliances with a number of European and Asian firms. It routinely places some of its foreign employees on work rotations outside of their home countries to familiarize them with the corporation's technological capabilities and to benefit from their knowledge as well. Multinational oil companies, global construction firms, and other businesses do the same.

Eventually these employees return to their home countries. In some cases they will have a unique set of cross-cultural "demons" to contend with. A foreign employee who has worked outside their own country for a multinational firm will often return home with a tremendous amount of knowledge that they did not have when they left, and a newly acquired cultural overlay. If the employee's domestic operation [the corporation's overseas branch] cannot make use of their newfound knowledge, and therefore cannot challenge them on the job, where can they go? If there is a large technical disparity between the same industries in the two countries, these employees may feel that they have been dealt a bad hand. This problem usually surfaces when Western corporations establish a presence in third-world countries and employ local labor. The locals learn valuable skills that are useful only within the context of their job. These skills are acquired in-country, although workers are sometimes moved from their passport country to the country where their employer's headquarters are located. If the corporation then moves their operation to another country or simply closes it down because it was temporary to begin with, where can those skilled employees go to seek meaningful employment?

Many multinationals encounter the unique problem of the third-culture employee, as one oil company executive explains:

> We had a small operation in a South American country. One of the local geologists there was quite talented, and he was selected for, and placed in, a position in another country—not the United States. He was there for several years, but eventually his assignment ended and it was time for him to go home. Unfortunately, by that time we had shut down the operation in his country.
>
> So here's the question: Do we return him to his home country, and therefore cast him adrift, unemployed, as a thank you for his years of service? Do we leave him in-country, and try to find another position for him there? Or do we bring him back to the U.S. and force him and his family to swap cultures again? In my mind, the corporation had more than an employer-employee relationship with the man; it had a moral responsibility to take

care of him and his family. Of course, that belief complicated things dramatically.[4]

Multinationals should counsel these employees carefully before they accept such a position, and should have a contingency plan for the placement of the employee should such an eventuality take place. They should also discuss the situation with the employee and with the home department to make them aware of the challenges that the employee will encounter when they return. Some multinationals employ professional counselors to help third-country nationals (TCNs) manage their transition.[5]

In Japan, multinational business activity has created a cultural problem of some significance. According to Doug Rice, a sociologist in Boston who prepares Japanese jurors for the significant cultural jolt of testifying in the American court system, Japanese employees who work in the United States create problems when they return home:

> In the overly structured, highly stylized society of modern Japan, individuals are like soap bubbles. They slip and slide against one another in a completely frictionless fashion, behavior that is reflected in the *zaibatsu*, the modern business model of the country.

> When employees of Japanese firms are sent to the U.S. to take on assignments there, they return with

"rough edges" that disrupt the traditional smoothness of the social structure and prevent them from reintegrating easily. The social implications of reentry for a Japanese are quite profound because of the significant cultural differences that exist between Japan and the U.S.

Schoolchildren often suffer the most: Because they assimilate western behaviors, wear western dress, and speak improperly inflected Japanese, they are often targets of ridicule and ostracism when they return to Japan and enroll in school.

Multinationals beware: Reverse culture shock is not a uniquely American phenomenon. It affects anyone who crosses cultural boundaries.

Whatever the reason for an employee's selection for an overseas assignment, several observations must be made. First, the employee's intangible qualities are just as important as their work skills and experience, and must be assessed with equal weight. Second, those very qualities—age, experience, skill sets—can serve to either lessen the impact of repatriation or make the task infinitely harder. The young, inexperienced employee may have a stronger and more immediate need for a mentor than a more seasoned employee who is at least familiar with basic corporate culture and internal politics. On the other hand, the more mature employee may have greater concerns about longevity and continued employment. As a result, the mentor's job can be equally crucial for the older employee.

some lessons from them. We also listened to 'the pioneers'—the first few instructors who went to Australia and brought back experiences that we could take advantage of. We're still pretty new at the international stuff, but we're assembling a set of tools that we can use to manage our overseas people."

One of those tools is a worksheet that employees who return from an overseas assignment are required to fill out. When the form is complete, a meeting is scheduled with the corporation's management team to discuss the employee's comments and suggestions.

A sample form is shown on page 201.

Keys to Managing the Expatriate Employee

A successful expatriate employee management strategy addresses issues encountered in four key management areas: corporate rationale; preparation for departure; in-country issues; and repatriation. These issues are covered in detail in the following checklist.

Corporate Rationale

Design an official, well-defined expatriate philosophy.

Ensure that the philosophy is understood, supported, and used by both line management and human resources personnel. Take pains to balance the requirements and stipulations of both groups. Both are important: Line management is concerned with assurance of technical competence and the employee's ability to perform on the job, while human resources must properly assess, select, and support the employee.

Clearly define the corporate rationale for sending people overseas.

Create a well-thought-out program that reflects the corporate philosophy in the selection criteria. Use rational business reasons for selection of employees, but incorporate human judgment criteria as well. Match the reasons used to choose an expatriate employee with the requirements of the business plan.

Design a program in which the expatriation plan and the repatriation plan closely mirror each another. Keep in mind that the belief that the employee is "coming home" from an overseas assignment is inherently flawed: They are actually leaving home and entering a new culture. Make sure that the program reflects this and is sensitive to its implications.

Take steps to ensure that the rationale (and the attendant selection process) are consistent with organizational structure.

If employees are sent overseas as part of a managerial seasoning process, ensure that they are properly integrated upon their return. Create temporary assignments for them so that their newfound skills are immediately put to good use. If the employee is selected because of specific skills or capabilities, make sure that there are resources to help them

(Continued on p. 203)

Hill Associates Expatriate Follow-Up Program

Ref: GCK
Kuala Lumpur, 4/22/96–6/1/97

Dear Gary:

Welcome home! You recently returned from an extended assignment in Malaysia. As a corporation, we feel that the experiences you had in that country and the skills you developed while over there make you a uniquely valuable employee. International business is a growing component of our corporate strategy, and as a consequence of that we would like to ask you to complete this exercise.

Please answer the following questions as completely and thoughtfully as you can. Your answers will benefit you as an employee because the information you tell us about yourself and your experiences while abroad will help us determine the best possible job for you. The information will also help Hill Associates develop better international business strategies, since it will (1) provide us with a discrete understanding of the business climate in Malaysia that can only be achieved through extensive in-country immersion, and (2) teach us how to most effectively manage our growing base of expatriate employees.

This form is provided in electronic format so that you can simply add your comments to it. When you are finished, please e-mail the completed form to _____.

1. Think back to the domestic job you held and the responsibilities you had before you accepted this most recent overseas position. Based on what you remember, what new skills have you acquired as a result of your overseas assignment? List as many as you can, irrespective of how trivial they may seem.

2. Of those skills, which are the most important to you personally? That is to say, which ones make you feel the most proud or accomplished for having acquired them? Why?
3. Which of those skills is most important today to Hill Associates? Which will be the most important next year? Why?
4. What was the best thing about working overseas? The worst? Why?
5. Please describe qualitatively the level of communication you had with the office in Colchester. Was it adequate? Too much? Not enough? How could the communication be improved? Did you feel disconnected from headquarters?
6. This is an open-ended question. Based on what you now know about the Malaysian marketplace, what steps should Hill Associates be taking today to improve their presence in-country that they may not be aware of? What major changes or trends are under way that might not be obvious to casual visitors or instructors who visit the country only briefly?
7. To help us improve the manner in which management interacts with its offshore employees, please complete the following question: "My life in Malaysia would have been made dramatically better if management had only..."
8. Write a paragraph that describes your ideal job back at headquarters. Note: This does not have to be a position that currently exists.
9. Which organization at Hill Associates are you most ideally suited to work in, given your new skill set? Why?
10. Please list any other observations, comments, or suggestions that would help Hill Associates improve its overseas presence and the manner in which it interacts with and manages its overseas personnel. Please be as complete as possible.

> Thank you for taking the time to do this. As soon as we have reviewed your comments and suggestions, we will schedule a meeting to discuss and act upon them.
>
> Welcome home!

maintain technical currency while abroad. Provide assessment exercises that will help employees and their families assess their suitability for an overseas assignment prior to entering the corporate selection process (see Appendix).

Clearly define the selection criteria for potential expatriate employees.

Make sure that the process takes into account such intangible qualities as suitability for expatriate assignment, acculturation capability, and maturity, in addition to job performance and individual work ethics. *Guarantee that job security is assured, if applicable.*

The expatriate often feels isolated when abroad and separated from the goings-on at corporate headquarters. Build processes that guarantee that they are at least kept apprised of job availability. Ensure that the mentor helps the expatriate prepare for job re-entry, updates their résumé, and so forth.

Create a dedicated expatriate orientation and training program to prepare the employee for their assignment. Conversely, create a similar program to assist with repatriation.

Ensure that the expatriation and repatriation plans align. To the employee, the rigors of expatriation and repatriation are very similar, and they must therefore be treated similarly.

Appoint a mentor for each overseas employee.

A mentor program is one of the most powerful tools a corporation can use to ease the challenges of managing a multinational workforce. Described in Part 3, mentor programs, if managed well, provide both the employee and the corporation with the necessary link between the domestic workforce and the home office. The mentors must be carefully selected and the program well thought out and managed, but the end result can be an ideal development environment for both the expatriate employee and the global human resources organization.

Empower the mentor to make decisions that are in the best interests of the expatriate. Ensure that there is high-level corporate support for the program and for the mentor. Recognize the scope of the mentor's responsibilities, and structure their job accordingly.

Preparation for Departure

Formalize a letter of understanding that clearly defines expectations on the part of both the individual and the company. Design a clear process that details exactly what the employee will do upon their return.

Avoid surprises by drafting a formal letter of understanding between the employee and the corporation. The memo should detail agreed-upon expectations, consequences for success and failure, length of the assignment, the employee's position upon their return, and compensation details. Define a clearly articulated, written compensation plan for expatriates. Define how salaries are to be adjusted, what intangible add-ons are to be provided by the corporation, and when incentive allowances are to be paid. Clearly define when add-on salary components will end. Use corporate or professional financial advisors and social counselors to work with the employee prior to departure regarding the "traps" of expatriate living. Provide them with suggested strategies for investment of excess income.

Make cultural sensitivity training available.

Prior to departure and the return home, provide the employee and his or her family with information about cultural expectations. This can be delivered in as simple a form as local newspapers and meetings with former expatriates, or as formal as immersive, full-time training.

Make language training available.

Even a few weeks of training to familiarize the ear with the sounds of a new language can be extremely valuable. Fluency is best achieved in-country.

Provide transition training for the employee's family, particularly the children.

Do not overlook the family. Be mindful of the fact that the employee's success is directly related to the family's successful transition.

In-Country Issues

Understand how disparate business practices are to be managed.

For example, in countries where business/labor partnerships are radically different, establish guidelines that define how much leeway the expatriate manager has within which to operate. Research and use available resources (see the Appendix for a selection of such resources).

Clearly define how much freedom the expatriate employee has to operate within the legal strictures of the host country [Foreign Corrupt Practices Act (FCPA), for example].

Leave nothing to chance. Educate the employee and ensure that they understand the options available to them. Arrange for new expatriates to spend time with experienced expatriates.

Create a process to manage the severe disparity that usually exists between stateside and expatriate employees with regard to scope of responsibilities.

Expatriates often have significantly more fiscal leeway and decision-making power than their domestic counterparts. When they return to a domestic position, they often feel unchallenged by the far more bureaucratic and rigidly structured environment to which they return.

Communicate organizational changes to the expatriate employee in order to ensure that they are kept abreast of goings-on within their own company.

Use whatever means are available to keep the employee in the corporate information loop: regular and corporate mail, e-mail, Internet access, video conferences, teleconferences, enforced home leave, training, etc.

Repatriation

Use the knowledge of returned expatriates.

Above all else, take steps to ensure that returning expatriate employees do not end up in positions that fail to use the considerable skills that they acquire during their overseas assignment.

Create plans/functions that help ease the transition of the employee's family.

Create an equally robust family repatriation program. Rely on the experience of other returned expatriates as well as on professional guidance services.

MANAGING THE EXPATRIATE EMPLOYEE: A CHECKLIST FOR SUCCESS

The following is a summary of the points covered in this chapter.

Corporate Rationale

Design an official, well-defined expatriate philosophy.

Clearly define the corporate rationale for sending people overseas.

Take steps to ensure that the rationale and the attendant selection process are consistent with organizational structure.

Clearly define the selection criteria for potential expatriate employees.

Create a dedicated expatriate orientation and training program to prepare the employee for their assignment. Conversely, create a similar program to assist with repatriation.

Preparation for Departure

Formalize a letter of understanding that clearly defines expectations on the part of both the individual and the company. Design a clear process that details exactly what the employee will do upon their return.

Appoint a mentor for each overseas employee.

Make cultural sensitivity training available.

Make language training available.

Provide transition training for the employee's family, particularly the children.

Clearly articulate how differences (salary, benefits, taxes, etc.) are to be accounted for.

Guarantee that job security is assured, if applicable.

Take pains to ensure that disparities in compensation between domestic and expatriate positions are clearly understood by the employee.

In-Country Issues

Understand how disparate business practices are to be managed.

Clearly define how much freedom the expatriate employee has to operate within the legal strictures of the host country.

Create a process to manage the severe disparity that usually exists between stateside and expatriate employees with regard to scope of responsibility.

Communicate organizational changes to the expatriate employee.

Repatriation

Create and rely on a mentor program.

Use the skills of experienced repatriate employees to place the returned employee and reduce the difficulties of cross-cultural transition.

Conduct transition workshops.

Place the employee properly upon their return to the passport country.

Create plans/functions that help ease the transition of the employee's family.

Educate home office personnel about the unique skills that the arriving employee brings and the challenges they will face during the repatriation phase of reentry.

Summary

Because of the globalization of the modern marketplace, it is critical that the corporation design a business plan that addresses not only the issues associated with running a multinational workforce but also the assessment, selection, placement, support, management, compensation, preparation, repatriation, and domestic reassimilation of employees who work offshore.

In addition to the resources that most corporations can muster internally to accomplish this task, there are many support agencies that specialize in the challenges of the multinational workplace. Regardless of whether the corporation uses internal or external support structures, it must build an infrastructure that recognizes and honors the unique environment that faces employees who work overseas, and that places appropriate value on their specialized skills by creating a job that uses those skills when they return.

Questions for Review

1. List the three factors that HR professionals cite as the most common sources of difficulties for expatriates. Which do you believe has the most impact? The least? Why?

2. Is it possible to eliminate the challenges of cross-cultural transition? Why or why not?

3. What kind of information can be made available electronically to expatriates? Why is this medium often more effective than traditional methods of delivering information?

4. What specific activities might help familiarize domestic employees with goings-on in the overseas work environment?

5. In some companies foreign compensation packages are quite lucrative and can lead to problems when employees express a desire to stay abroad rather than return home at the end of their assignment. How might this issue be dealt with most effectively?

6. In addition to those described in the chapter, what tools and techniques can be employed to help employees maintain their technical currency?

7. Why is the feedback loop so important in a multinational managerial environment? How can it be made most effective?

Notes

1. From an article in the *Burlington Free Press*, date unknown.

2. A set of satirical observations, including "Work expands to fill the time available for its completion."

3. Name changed by request.

4. The employee eventually accepted a position in the United States and has done exceptionally well. Both he and his family have adjusted very well to life in a new country. This is not always the case, however.

5. See "Resource: Consultants for International Living," p. 111.

Conclusion

In the twenty-first century the number of companies with an international presence will grow dramatically, and with their growth will come an increase in the number of employees working in foreign countries. Those people will spend time abroad, become adjusted to life there, and manage their companies' affairs in a transnational environment. Eventually they will return home.

These employees have served as corporate representatives and cultural liaisons between the domestic corporation and the host country for a considerable amount of time. They are good at it, proud of their accomplishments, and willing to do what they can to further the company's goals.

It has cost the corporation a quarter of a million dollars or more a year to have each employee in-country, but presumably the cost is justified by a lucrative return on the investment.

When these specialized employees return, their value to the corporation does not have to diminish. The company's growing international presence dictates that domestic employees' levels of understanding and involvement in the firm's international ventures should increase steadily. Who better to facilitate that growing awareness than employees who have lived it?

By placing returned expatriates in positions that reduce the gap between the domestic and international segments of the corporation, several agendas are served. First, the domestic employees benefit, because they become attuned to the strategic importance of the organization's operations abroad. Second, the expatriates benefit, because they fulfill a necessary role in the corporation. Finally, the company as a whole wins, because it has realized a profit not only from its overseas operations but from its overseas employees as well.

The information presented in this book cannot eliminate the problems and challenges of cross-cultural transition, but it can significantly reduce them if implemented as part of a well-designed and carefully thought out expatriate management policy.

Bibliography

Adler, Nancy J. *International Dimensions of Organizational Behavior,* 2nd ed. Belmont, CA: Wadsworth, 1991.

Aitken, Thomas. *The Multinational Man: The Role of the Manager Abroad.* New York: Halsted Press, Wiley, 1973.

Austin, Clyde. *Cross-Cultural Reentry: A Book of Readings.* Abilene, TX: Abilene Christian University Press, 1987.

———. *Cross-Cultural Reentry: An Annotated Bibliography.* Abilene, TX: Abilene Christian University Press, 1983.

Bachler, Christopher J. "Global Inpats—Don't Let Them Surprise You." *Personnel Journal,* June 1996.

Ball, Donald A., and Wendell H. McCulloch, Jr. *International Business: Introduction and Essentials.* Plano, TX: Business Publications, 1982.

Eakin, Kay Branaman. *The Foreign Service Teenager—At Home in the U.S.: A Few Thoughts for Parents Returning with Teenagers.* Overseas Briefing Center, Foreign Service Institute, U.S. Department of State, May 1988.

Cagney, W. F. "Executive Reentry: The Problem of Repatriation." *Personnel Journal,* 1975, 54 (9), 487–488.

Craighead Country Reports. Various issues from the 1996 series. Darien, CT: Craighead Publications.

Culturgram, various issues from the 1996 series. Provo, UT: David M. Kennedy Center for International Studies, Brigham Young University.

Freedman, A. "A Strategy for Managing 'Cultural' Transitions: Reentry from Training." In *The 1980 Annual Handbook for Group Facilitators,* edited by J. W. Pfeiffer and J. E. Jones. San Diego: University Associates, 1980.

Faulkner, R. R., and D. B. McGraw. *Uneasy Homecoming: Stages in the Reentry Transition of Vietnam Veterans. Urban Life,* 1977, 6 (3), 303-328.

Gedvilas, Cathy. "Examining Expatriate Relocation Costs and Benefits." *ACA News,* September 1996.

Global Relocation Trends 1995 Survey Report. Sponsored by Windham International and the National Foreign Trade Council, December 1995.

Hartzel, Nedra. *The Impact of a Transition Workshop on Reentry Anxiety of Peace Corps Volunteers.* Ph. D. diss., University of Maryland, 1991.

International Sourcing and Selection Practices 1995 Survey Report. New York: National Foreign Trade Council and SRI Selection Research International, September 1995.

Iyer, Pico. *Video Night in Kathmandu and Other Reports from the Not-So-Far-East.* New York: Vintage Departures, 1988.

Jenkins, Larry. "Overseas Assignments: Sending the Right People." *International HR Journal,* Summer 1995.

Kalb, Rosalind, and Penelope Welch. *Moving Your Family Overseas.* Yarmouth, ME: Intercultural Press, 1992.

Kendall, D. W. *Repatriation: An Ending and a Beginning.* In *Business Horizons,* Bloomington: Indiana University Graduate School of Business, November-December 1981.

Kinsey Goman, Carol. *Managing in a Global Organization: Keys to Success in a Changing World.* Menlo Park, CA: Crisp Publications, 1994.

Moran, Robert T., and Jeffrey Abbott. *NAFTA: Managing the Cultural Differences.* Houston: Gulf Publishing, 1994.

Noer, David M. *Multinational People Management—A Guide for Organizations and Employees.* Washington, DC: Bureau of National Affairs, 1975.

McCluskey, Karen Curnow, ed. *Notes from a Traveling Childhood: Readings for Internationally Mobile Parents and*

Children. Washington, DC: Foreign Service Youth Foundation, 1994.

Prencipe, Loretta. "How to Import Network Specialists." *Network World,* September 9, 1996.

Purcer-Smith, Gillian. *Studies of International Mobility*. New York: National Foreign Trade Council, 1971.

Raimy, Eric. "Repat Roulette." *Human Resource Executive,* November 1994, pp 51–54.

Robock, Stefan H., Kenneth Simmonds, and Jack Zwick. *International Business and Multinational Enterprises.* Homewood, IL: Richard D. Irwin, 1977.

Smith, Carolyn D. *The Absentee American: Repatriates' Perspectives on America*. Bayside, NY: Aletheia Publications, 1994.

Swaak, Reyer A. "Today's Expatriate Family: Dual Careers and Other Obstacles." *Compensation and Benefits Review,* January–February 1995.

———. "Expatriate Failures: Too Many, Too Much Cost, Too Little Planning." *Compensation and Benefits Review,* November–December 1995.

Wagner, Kenneth, and Tony Magistrale. *Writing Across Culture.* New York: Peter Lang Publishing, 1995.

Wallach, Joel, and Gale Metcalf. "The Hidden Problem of Reentry." *The Bridge,* Winter 1980.

Wederspahn, Gary M. "Controlling the Costs of Expatriate Assignments." *Journal of International Compensation and Benefits,* January–February 1995.

Werkman, Sidney. *Bringing Up Children Overseas: A Guide for Families*. New York: Basic Books, 1977.

———. "Coming Home: Adjustment of Americans to the United States After Living Abroad." From *Uprooting and Development: Dilemmas of Coping with Modernization,* edited by G. V. Coelho and P. I. Ahmed. New York: Plenum Press, 1980.

Glossary

acculturation: The modification of the culture of a group or an individual as a result of contact with a different culture.

argot: A specialized vocabulary or set of idioms used by a particular group.

Coordinating Committee on Export Controls (CoCom): The U.S. Senate subcommittee that governs the export of certain trade items to select countries. For example, high-tech materials such as computer chips and other components are often prohibited from being exported to certain countries in the Middle East.

cyberspace: A word that describes the evolving communications culture that revolves around the Internet and other forms of electronic communication.

EC *See* European Community

electronic mail (e-mail): Messages that are transmitted electronically.

erosion, intellectual: The problem that occurs when technical employees reside in countries where the level of technical capability is limited or where they are isolated from the sources of information that allow them to keep their knowledge current.

ethnocentrism: Belief in the superiority of one's own ethnic group.

European Community: The trading bloc formed by the economic union of member European nations.

expat: Abbreviation for *expatriate*.

expatriate: A person who has taken up residence in a foreign country.

expatriosis: The set of problems that a returned expatriate encounters after being back in the passport country following an extended stay abroad (author's term).

FCPA *See* Foreign Corrupt Practices Act

finance, multinational: The special form of finance that must take into account the complexity and intricacies involved in conducting business at multinational levels.

firefighting assignment: An assignment undertaken by an employee whose specific skills are required to resolve a particular task.

Foreign Corrupt Practices Act: The set of laws governing proper business conduct by American corporations doing business in other countries. The FCPA specifically prohibits any business practice that would be illegal in the United States, even if it is admissible under the laws of the host country.

funds, repatriation of: The process by which profits earned in a multinational business are returned to the domestic corporation.

General Agreement on Tariffs and Trade (GATT) *See* World Trade Organization

geocentric: A perspective that is globally centered rather than being centered around one's own country.

getting (your) ticket punched: A phrase used to describe the requirement by some companies that employees accept at least one international assignment as part of a "seasoning" process.

globalization: A term used to describe the increasingly international nature of business in the world today.

global nomad: Anyone who had an internationally mobile childhood due to their parents' work. They are neither of their parents' culture nor of the cultures in which they lived, but some combination, which forms a third culture. *See also* third culture kids

hardship pay: Additional remuneration paid to individuals who work in locations with living conditions that are substantially inferior to those the employee would encounter at home. These might be third world countries, countries at war, and the like. Also called *hazard pay* or *swamp pay*.

hegemony: The predominant influence of one state over others.

hegira: A flight to escape danger. In this case, used to describe the flight of expatriate employees from their original employer.

hemorrhage, intellectual: The loss of skilled people from a multinational corporation because of improper management of those people. Reasons include failure to recognize their capabilities and value to the company, failure to challenge them intellectually, and the like.

hyperinflation: Extremely high monetary inflation.

international: Of, relating to, or involving two or more nations.

mentor: An employee who is responsible for helping to manage the affairs of an expatriate employee in order to keep them in the "corporate loop."

missionary kids (MKs): Children of missionary parents who were raised abroad.

multinational: A corporation that has operations in more than one country.

NAFTA *See* North American Free Trade Agreement

nationalize: To convert from private to governmental ownership and control.

North American Free Trade Agreement (NAFTA): The recently formed trade pact between Mexico, Canada, and the United States.

offshore: A business that is located or based in a foreign country and not subject to local tax laws. Often used to describe the foreign operations of a domestic corporation.

Parkinson's Law: A set of satirical observations, such as "Work expands to fill the time available for its completion."

passport country: An individual's native country, and therefore the issuer of the individual's passport.

reentry: The process of returning to the country of origin. Sometimes called *repatriation*.

repatriate: To return to the country of birth, citizenship, or origin.

show-off factor: The tendency of returned expatriates to brag about their experiences abroad. While a certain amount of this behavior may be bragging, it is often an expression of pride in having lived and succeeded overseas. The tendency to talk about experiences abroad is occasionally misinterpreted as bragging.

snail mail: Standard mail, as opposed to the far faster e-mail.

sponsor *See* mentor

third culture adults (TCAs): Adults reared in one culture, working for a company from a second culture, and physically located in a third culture. Or, adults who have lived and worked in a variety of international venues, who then return home to a "third culture."

third culture kids (TCKs): Individuals who had an internationally mobile childhood because of their parents' work. The term stems from the fact that they are neither of their parents' culture nor of the cultures in which they lived, but some combination. Hence the term *third culture*.

third world countries: Underdeveloped or developing countries, especially those not allied with Communist countries.

transnational: Reaching beyond or transcending national boundaries. Often used to describe the activities of corporations that operate in multiple countries.

video teleconference: Similar to a standard telephone conference call between multiple sites, but with the addition of video. During a video teleconference the individuals taking part can see all other sites, although not necessarily simultaneously.

water cooler effect: The intangible, subliminal, osmotic manner in which co-workers share information by simply talking to one another, overhearing conversations, reading intracompany memos, and so forth.

World Trade Organization (WTO): The newest large-scale global trade organization, currently comprising the United States, Canada, and the members of the EC.

zaibatsu: A Japanese conglomerate or cartel.

Appendix

Organization List

For additional information, please contact the following organizations:

Air Animal®
4120 West Cypress Street
Tampa, FL 33607

Air Animal provides pet transportation services for expatriate families, including animal health certification, country intelligence, physical preparation and shipment, quarantine, and a variety of other services.

Consultants for International Living
200 W. 57th Street, Suite 1310
New York, NY 10019
212-265-6722

CIL is an independent consulting firm serving the needs of multinational corporations, their employees, and families at all phases of the international assignment process, from selection through repatriation.

Craighead Publications Inc.
P.O. Box 1253
Darien, CT 06820

Craighead publishes country intelligence reports that include living information, financial and economic data, cultural information, and business practices.

Employee Relocation Council
1720 N Street, NW
Washington, DC 20036

ERC is a professional membership organization that addresses domestic and international corporate relocation by providing information in the areas of relocation policies and trends, tax and legal issues, and professional development and networking. It also issues a number of publications, including *Mobility* magazine.

Foreign Service Youth Foundation
P.O. Box 39185
Washington, DC 20016

The Foreign Service Youth Foundation provides repatriation support services for children returning from overseas assignments.

Global Nomads International
2001 O St., NW
Washington, DC 20036
202-466-2244

Global Nomads International is a not-for-profit organization dedicated to providing a forum for affirmation of the value of an internationally mobile childhood by joining other global nomads in sharing experiences and ideas; for exploration of the lifelong impact of this experience through discussions, conferences, workshops, publications, and tapes; and for action to apply intercultural and linguistic skills, global awareness, and appreciation of diversity.

Intercultural Press, Inc.
P.O. Box 700
Yarmouth, ME 04096

Intercultural Press publishes books, videotapes, games, and exercises that focus on cross-cultural interaction—the interaction of people who come from different cultural backgrounds. This focus includes domestic (interracial, interethnic) as well as international cross-cultural relations.

Kennedy Center Publications
Brigham Young University
280 Herald R. Clark Building
P.O. Box 24538
Provo, UT 84602

Kennedy Center Publications publishes *Culturgrams,* culture-specific country briefings for a wide range of countries.

National Foreign Trade Council
1270 Avenue of the Americas
New York, NY 10020

The NFTC is a nonprofit organization that has as its primary objectives the promotion of an open trading system, expansion of exports, and policies to help U.S. businesses compete effectively in global markets.

Overseas Brats
P.O. Box 29805
San Antonio, TX 78229
210-349-1394

Overseas Brats provides a centralized registry of international high school graduates to facilitate communication among peers.

NFATC/Overseas Briefing Center
4000 Arlington Boulevard
Room E2121, SA-42
Arlington, VA 22204
703-302-7268

The Overseas Briefing Center provides a wide range of support services for U.S. government employees and their families who are anticipating a return, or returning from overseas assignments. Its services include seminars, workshops, orientation exercises, and useful publications.

Overseas Schools Combined Alumni Registry (OSCAR)
P.O. Box 7763
Washington, DC 20044

OSCAR is a combined registry of graduate information for schools located overseas.

Prudential Relocation Global Services
200 Summit Lake Drive
Valhalla, NY 10595

Prudential Relocation offers thirty years of experience in global relocation and business consulting, and helps make the most of costly international human resources investments.

Society for Intercultural Education, Training, and Research (SIETAR)
808 17th Street NW, Suite 200
Washington, DC 20006

SIETAR conducts research and publishes information on transnational awareness.

Useful Contacts

Air Ambulance, Inc.	800-284-8300
American Red Cross	202-737-8300
Berlitz Language Centers	202-331-1160
Federal Centers for Disease Control and Prevention (CDC)	404-332-4559
David M. Kennedy International Center	801-378-6528
Inlingua School of Languages	202-289-8666
International Center for Language Studies	202-639-8800
Linguex	202-296-1112
Passport office	202-647-0518
U.S. Customs Service	202-927-6724
Intercultural Communication Institute (ICI)	503-297-4622
School for International Training	802-258-3267

Online Resources

Many organizations host World Wide Web sites or e-mail response services that can be accessed using browsers such as Netscape or Explorer. The amount of accessible information is astounding (a recent study observed that the number of network-reachable WWW information servers doubles every 57 days!) and is a powerful tool for expatriate employees. Equally useful are online search tools such as Yahoo (www.yahoo.com) and AltaVista (www.altavista.com), which dramatically simplify the information search process.

The list that follows is far from complete and is included to provide starting points for more detailed search routines.

Global Nomads International
www.gni.org

Information SuperLibrary
www.mcp.com

Intercultural Communication Institute
ici@intercultural.org

Language Sites
www.cc.utah.edu/~coj6886/jltc.html

National Technical Information Service (NTIS)
www.fedworld.gov/ntis

School for International Training
www.worldlearning.org/sit.html

Smithsonian Institution
www.si.edu

Stat-USA
www.stat-usa.gov

United Nations
www.un.org

MapQuest
www.mapquest.com

International Newspapers
www.potter.net/mediasite/international.html

Worldwide Language Institute
wwli.com/index.html

Federal Centers for Disease Control
www.cdc.gov

Central Intelligence Agency World Factbook
www.odci.cia.gov

National Archives
www.nara.gov

Peace Corps
www.clark.net/pub/peace/PeaceCorps.html

Permissions

Excerpt from *American Heritage Dictionary,* Third Edition, used with permission of Houghton-Mifflin. Copyright 1996 by Houghton Mifflin Company. Reprinted by permission from *The American Heritage Dictionary of the English Language,* Third Edition.

Excerpt from Gillian Purcer-Smith, *Studies of International Mobility,* used with permission of the National Foreign Trade Council.

Excerpt from Eric Raimy, "Repat Roulette," used with permission of *Human Resource Executive Magazine.* Copyright 1994.

Excerpt from John Steinbeck, *Cannery Row.* Copyright 1945 by John Steinbeck. Renewed copyright 1973 by Elaine Steinbeck, John Steinbeck IV, and Thom Steinbeck. Used with permission of Viking Penguin, a division of Penguin Books USA Inc.

Except from NFTC, *International Sourcing and Selection Practices,* September 1995, and *Global Relocation Trends 1995 Survey Report,* used with permission of the National Foreign Trade Council.

Excerpt from Kay Branaman Eakin, *The Foreign Service Teenager—At Home in the U.S.,* used with permission of the Overseas Briefing Center, Foreign Service Institute, U.S. Department of State.

Excerpt from Sara Mansfield Taber, *Longing for America: Notes from a Traveling Childhood,* used with permission of the author and the Foreign Service Youth Foundation.

Excerpt from Ruth Useem, "Third Culture Kids," *Today's Education,* September-October 1976, used with permission.

Excerpt from Peter Drucker, *People and Performance,* used with permission of Harper and Row. Copyright 1977.

Excerpt from Pico Iyer, *Video Night in Kathmandu and Other Tales from the Not-So-Far East,* used with permission of Random House, Inc. Copyright 1989.

Index

acceptance, 66, 67, 95, 98, 103, 179
acculturation, 13, 19, 23, 44, 66, 67, 80, 110, 203, 219
age, 46, 141, 152, 155, 198
Air Animàl,® 86
Alagna, Frank, 112
American School of Madrid, 2, 3, 7, 8
appliances, 91
assessment, 13, 19, 40, 41, 44, 47, 49, 52, 59, 69, 82, 111, 179, 203, 211
AT&T, 39, 74, 75, 76, 79, 121, 122, 175
Avon Products, 28
balloon payment, 178
Basic Organization of Associated Labor (BOAL), 171, 185
Better Business Bureau, 116
birth certificates, 90
bribery, 186
Brigham Young University, 194, 216, 226
Bryson, Bill, 11
budget, family, 116
business practices, 17, 160, 161, 162, 164, 174, 192, 206, 209, 225
Campbell, Eric, 28
CDC, 89, 228
chat groups, 115
Chicano, 148
churches, 54, 56, 58, 90, 96
Close of Service Conference, 176
closure, 111
CoCOM, 30
colonialism, 16
colonists, 16
communication, 98, 202, 219, 226
compensation, 19, 38, 42, 70, 75, 79, 164, 178, 179, 180, 181, 205, 209, 211, 212

Consultants for International Living (CIL), 111, 112, 113, 176, 197, 224
continuity, 43, 150
Craighead Country Reports, 190, 191, 216
cultural chameleons, 139
cultural sponges, 139
culture shock, 5, 24, 30, 67, 153, 159, 160, 161, 175, 198
Culturgrams, 189, 194, 226
Customs Service, 228
cyberspace, 72, 219
Dargy, Cathleen, 74
David M. Kennedy Center for International Studies, 190, 194, 216
Eakin, Kay Branaman, 67, 144, 216, 234
Eastern Bloc, 3
Eastman Kodak, 101
European Community (EC), 28, 158, 219, 223
electronic mail, 72, 75, 219, 222
Employee Relocation Council, 81, 225
Europe, 2, 9, 25, 72, 111, 119, 187
exile syndrome, 73
expatriation, 6, 61, 65, 66, 71, 83, 92, 93, 104, 110, 193, 200, 204
expatriosis, 5
family stability, 61, 62
feedback, 110, 170, 212
firefighting role, 187
fiscal responsibilities, 164, 186
Five Cs, 149
Foreign Corrupt Practices Act (FCPA), 184, 206, 220
Fortune 500, 18
GATT, 28, 220
Global Nomads International, 7, 11, 133, 134, 136, 137, 138, 141, 149, 221, 225, 229
globalization, 30, 211, 220
going native, 109
Hanley, Jerry, 39
hardship pay, 178, 222
hardship post, 3, 179
hazard pay, 178
health, 2, 37, 45, 53, 56, 61, 86, 112, 152, 191, 224
health care products, 45
hegemony, 16, 221
hidden immigrants, 140

Index

home leave, 79, 98, 99, 100, 104, 109, 207
housing, 2, 24, 28, 83, 90, 127, 165, 181, 191
human resources, 5, 28, 38, 39, 40, 49, 51, 62, 67, 69, 73, 74, 75, 76, 88, 89, 91, 92, 104, 110, 113, 115, 120, 122, 123, 125, 127, 131, 153, 159, 164, 170, 193, 194, 199, 204, 211, 217, 227
IBM, 41, 195
Intercultural Press, 85, 189, 217, 226
Internet, 73, 165, 170, 188, 207, 219
Internet telephony, 165
Iyer, Pico, 11, 181, 217, 234
journal, 116
Journey Home Workshops, 111, 176
Latin America, 38, 160, 182
letter of understanding, 78, 79, 80, 88, 93, 179-180, 204, 205, 208
line management, 38, 39, 40, 51, 75, 91, 113, 199
Martin, Douglas, 188
maturity, 46, 61, 111, 203
McCaig, Norma, 137, 139, 149, 221
McDonald's International, 188
medical records, 89, 129
medications, 46, 89, 90
mentor, 70, 71, 72, 74, 75, 77, 78, 79, 88, 91, 107, 109, 110, 115, 116, 120, 121, 123, 125, 127, 131, 138, 163, 164, 168, 176, 182, 188, 198, 203, 204, 209, 221, 222
multinational corporation, 13, 16, 19, 20, 26, 29, 31, 41, 48, 49, 52, 69, 85, 111, 112, 149, 158, 182, 185, 195, 221, 224
NAFTA, 28, 158, 217, 221
National Foreign Trade Council (NFTC), 24, 35, 39, 41, 42, 49, 69, 217, 218, 226, 234
nationals, foreign, 75, 112, 136, 164, 195
office osmosis, 23
orientation, 19, 44, 65, 82, 95, 96, 97, 103, 128, 191, 203, 208, 227
Parkinson's Law, 178, 222
passport country, 7, 12, 22, 23, 25, 28, 45, 59, 71, 91, 99, 106, 108, 110, 128, 138, 140, 144, 148, 152, 161, 162, 180, 196, 210, 220, 222
Peace Corps, 11, 176, 217, 230
pets, 21, 86, 88
Philip Morris, 101
photographs, passport, 90

placement (following repatriation), 19, 39, 40, 42, 49, 109,
    110, 115, 176, 197, 211
placement services, 42
prescriptions, 89
Prudential Relocation Global Services, 82, 83, 227
realtors, 127
repatriates, 176
rescue, 28, 108, 110
résumé, 76, 79, 119, 121, 122, 203
reverse culture shock, 5, 24, 153, 159, 160, 161, 198
Rice, Doug, 197
Rip Van Winkle, 36, 106
salary shock, 180
salary treatment, 180
school, 3, 5, 8, 21, 23, 43, 44, 47, 57, 70, 80, 85, 87, 90, 96,
    102, 107, 112, 116, 128, 129, 138, 144, 147, 148, 149, 150,
    154, 184, 191, 198, 226, 227
selection, 13, 19, 26, 37, 38, 39, 40, 46, 48, 49, 50, 61, 62, 65,
    69, 82, 92, 111, 161, 198, 200, 203, 206, 208, 211, 224
Selection Research International (SRI), 35, 39, 69, 217
servants, 68, 103, 177
South America, 16, 172, 196
spouse, 21, 24, 37, 41, 42, 43, 44, 50, 55, 62, 76, 80, 91, 92, 96,
    101, 112, 117, 128
strategy, 13, 26, 36, 40, 70, 159, 163, 179, 199, 201
substance abuse, 45
supervision, 146
swamp pay, 178
talent inventory, 39
technical knowledge, 22, 120
teens, 68, 116, 128, 145, 155
Theroux, Paul, 11
third culture kid, 7, 133, 137, 221, 222
3M, 74, 101
toddlers, 142
toys, 89, 143, 150
trailing family, 21
trailing spouse, 96
transcripts, school, 90
transnationalists, 140
trip report, 122, 123, 131
University of Pennsylvania, 158
U.S. Department of Labor, 42
Useem, Ruth, 133

vacation, 23, 100, 117, 151
valuables, videotape of, 54, 56, 57, 89, 91, 129
Vikings, Norse, 16
water cooler effect, 22, 223
Web site, 73, 169, 229
Werkman, S. L., and Johnson, F., 134
Wharton School of Business, 158
Windham International, 42, 48, 49, 217
women's clubs, 102
work ethics, 37, 38, 203
world citizens, 141
World Trade Organization (WTO), 28, 158, 223
World Wide Web, 115, 116, 229
zaibatsu, 197

About the Author

Steven Shepard is a senior member of technical staff with Hill Associates in Colchester, Vermont. A professional writer and educator, Shepard specializes in international issues in telecommunications and the social implications of technological change. He received his B.A. in Spanish from the University of California at Berkeley, and his M.S. in international business from St. Mary's College. He is married and has two children.